GENETIC DISCRIMINATION

GENETIC DISCRIMINATION

LEANA J. ALBERTSON
EDITOR

Nova Science Publishers, Inc.
New York

For permission to use material from this book please contact us:
Telephone 631-231-7269; Fax 631-231-8175
Web Site: http://www.novapublishers.com

LIBRARY OF CONGRESS CATALOGING-IN-PUBLICATION DATA

Genetic discrimination / Leana J. Albertson, editor.
p. ; cm.
ISBN 978-1-60456-357-3 (hardcover)
1. Medical genetics--Law and legislation--United States. 2. Discrimination in employment--Law and legislation--United States. 3. Discrimination in insurance--Law and legislation--United States. 4. Genetic screeing--Government policy--United States. 5. Medical records--Access control--United States. I. Albertson, Leana J.
[DNLM: 1. Genetic Privacy--legislation & jurisprudence--United States. 2. Health Policy--United States. 3. Prejudice--United States. W 32.5 AA1 G328 2008]
KF3827.G4G453 2008
344.04'196--dc22

2007052109

Published by Nova Science Publishers, Inc. ✦ New York

CONTENTS

PREFACE

Genetic information can be misused. It can be used to discriminate against people in health insurance and employment. People known to carry a gene that increases their likelihood of developing cancer, for example, may get turned down for health insurance. Without health insurance, it may be impossible for some people to get treatment for a disease that could be fatal. This may lead some people to decide against genetic testing for fear of what the results might show, and who might find out about them. It also could lead some people to decline participation in biomedical research such as studies of gene mutations associated with certain diseases that examine the history of families prone to those maladies. This new book examines some of the hot areas of research in the field.

Chapter 1 - A key policy issue before Congress is whether the potential for genetic discrimination by employers and insurers merits protections for genetic information that are more extensive than those already in place for health information. For the stated purpose of prohibiting discrimination on the basis of genetic information with respect to health insurance and employment, the Genetic Information Nondiscrimination Act of 2007 (H.R. 493) was introduced in the House on January 16, 2007. On January 22, 2007, the act was introduced in the Senate (S. 358). The act is identical to the Genetic Information Nondiscrimination Act of 2005, which passed the Senate by a vote of 98-0 (S. 306, 109th). An identical House bill (H.R. 1227, 109th), never came to a vote. S. 306 was very similar to S. 1053 (108th), which the Senate passed in 2003 by a vote of 95-0. A distinct House bill, H.R. 1910 (108th), never came to a vote. This report focuses on the key points in the ongoing debate about genetic discrimination legislation.

S. 358 and H.R. 493 are supported by consumer groups, the medical profession, researchers, the medical products industry (including pharmaceutical companies), and President Bush, and are opposed primarily by the U.S. Chamber of Commerce. Since the first bills were introduced in the 103rd Congress, many of the arguments and positions supporting and opposing genetic nondiscrimination legislation have remained largely unchanged. Supporters of nondiscrimination legislation feel that current laws are not sufficient to protect individuals from discrimination in health insurance or employment. Supporters of the legislation further contend that without protection, individuals are hesitant to seek potentially beneficial genetic services or participate in much needed clinical research. Opponents believe that current law provides sufficient protection. They are primarily concerned that new legislation will provide further incentives and additional opportunities for litigation against employers.

Collectively, genetic diseases and common diseases with a genetic component pose a significant public health burden. With completion of the human genome sequence, scientists are now focusing on the development of clinical applications based on the sequence information. One such application, clinical genetic testing, is becoming available at a rapid rate, and some tests are beginning to be included in health insurance benefits packages. Genetic testing may both facilitate and be inhibited by the potential for genetic discrimination. Issues surrounding nondiscrimination addressed in this report include:

- What is health information and how is it currently used by health insurers and employers?
- What is genetic information?
- Is genetic information different from other health information?
- What evidence exists to suggest that discrimination is a problem?
- Would the proposed legislation be sufficient to protect "genetic information" and "genetic tests" that are of concern?

Chapter 2 - In the 109th Congress, several pieces of legislation were introduced that related to genetic and genomic technology and testing, including the Genetic Information Nondiscrimination Act of 2005 (S. 306/H.R. 1227), the Genomics and Personalized Medicine Act of 2006 (S. 3822) and the Prenatally Diagnosed Condition Awareness Act (S. 609). Although none of these bills passed, they signal the growing importance of the public policy issues surrounding the clinical and public health implications of new genetic technology. As genetic technologies proliferate and are increasingly used to guide clinical treatment, these public policy issues are likely to continue to garner considerable attention. Understanding the basic scientific concepts underlying genetics and genetic testing may help facilitate the development of more effective public policy in this area.

Most diseases have a genetic component. Some diseases such as Huntington's Disease are caused by a specific gene. Other diseases, such as heart disease and cancer, are caused by a complex combination of genetic and environmental factors. For this reason, the public health burden of genetic disease is substantial, as is its clinical significance. Experts note that society has recently entered a transition period in which specific genetic knowledge is becoming critical to the delivery of effective health care for everyone. Therefore, the value of and role for genetic testing in clinical medicine is likely to increase significantly in the future.

Chapter 3 - In April 2003, the finished sequence of the human genome was deposited into public databases. This milestone, which has been compared to the discoveries of Galileo, and other advances in genetics have created novel legal issues relating to genetic information. The Human Genome Project, which produced detailed maps of the 23 pairs of human chromosomes and sequenced 99% of the three billion nucleotide bases that make up the human genome, has been instrumental in the identification of genes implicated in various diseases including glaucoma, colon cancer, and cystic fibrosis. With the identification of these genes comes the hope of genetic therapies to cure disease but this scientific accomplishment is not without potential problems. For instance the presence of a cancer causing gene may indicate a predisposition but does not guarantee that the person will contract the disease: How should an employer or insurer respond? The ethical, social and legal implications of these technological advances have been the subject of significant scrutiny and concern.

The legal implications of such information have been addressed in various ways largely by states, but also by Congress. The Health Insurance Portability and Accountability Act of 1996, P.L. 104-191, is the first federal law to specifically address discrimination and insurance issues relating to genetic discrimination. Congress has considered several bills concerning genetics during the past several Congresses. In the 109th Congress, S. 306, the Genetic Information Nondiscrimination Act of 2005, was passed on February 17, 2005 by a vote of 98-0. A companion bill, H.R. 1227, was introduced on March 10, 2005. In the 108th Congress, the Senate passed the Genetic Information Nondiscrimination Act of 2003, S. 1053. H.R. 1910 was introduced in the House and hearings were held but the bill was not passed in the 108th Congress. This report discusses current federal law, state statutes, and legislation. It will be updated as needed.

Chapter 4 - H.R. 493, 110th Congress, the Genetic Information Nondiscrimination Act (GINA), passed the House on April 25, 2007. The Senate bill, S. 358, 110th Congress, was reported out of the Senate Health, Education, Labor, and Pensions Committee on March 29, 2007, and is currently awaiting Senate action. This report compares the provisions of H.R. 493 and S. 358 relating to GINA's prohibition of genetic discrimination in employment.

Chapter 6 - On April 25, the House passed the Genetic Information Nondiscrimination Act of 2007, H.R. 493, on a vote of 420-3. The Senate Health, Education, Labor, and Pensions (HELP) Committee approved similar legislation (S. 358). S. 358 is awaiting Senate floor action. The Genetic Information Nondiscrimination Act would restrict health insurers' (Title I) and employers' (Title II) acquisition and use of genetic information in several ways. These restrictions build upon those already imposed in federal law.

This report provides a comparison of the Title I provisions in H.R. 493 and S. 358. Those provisions would extend the current Health Insurance Portability and Accountability Act (HIPAA) protections against discrimination by group health plans and issuers of health insurance in both the group and individual markets, and restrict their collection, use and disclosure of genetic information. A separate CRS Report, RL33987, *Genetic Non-discrimination in Employment: A Comparison of Title II Provisions in S. 358 and H.R. 493, 110th Congress*, by Nancy Lee Jones, discusses the Title II employment provisions.

In: Genetic Discrimination
Editor: Leana J. Albertson, pp. 1-30

ISBN: 978-1-60456-357-3

Chapter 1

GENETIC DISCRIMINATION: OVERVIEW OF THE ISSUE AND PROPOSED LEGISLATION*

Erin D. Williams, Amanda K. Sarata and C. Stephen Redhead

ABSTRACT

A key policy issue before Congress is whether the potential for genetic discrimination by employers and insurers merits protections for genetic information that are more extensive than those already in place for health information. For the stated purpose of prohibiting discrimination on the basis of genetic information with respect to health insurance and employment, the Genetic Information Nondiscrimination Act of 2007 (H.R. 493) was introduced in the House on January 16, 2007. On January 22, 2007, the act was introduced in the Senate (S. 358). The act is identical to the Genetic Information Nondiscrimination Act of 2005, which passed the Senate by a vote of 98-0 (S. 306, 109th). An identical House bill (H.R. 1227, 109th), never came to a vote. S. 306 was very similar to S. 1053 (108th), which the Senate passed in 2003 by a vote of 95-0. A distinct House bill, H.R. 1910 (108th), never came to a vote. This report focuses on the key points in the ongoing debate about genetic discrimination legislation.

S. 358 and H.R. 493 are supported by consumer groups, the medical profession, researchers, the medical products industry (including pharmaceutical companies), and President Bush, and are opposed primarily by the U.S. Chamber of Commerce. Since the first bills were introduced in the 103rd Congress, many of the arguments and positions supporting and opposing genetic nondiscrimination legislation have remained largely unchanged. Supporters of nondiscrimination legislation feel that current laws are not sufficient to protect individuals from discrimination in health insurance or employment. Supporters of the legislation further contend that without protection, individuals are hesitant to seek potentially beneficial genetic services or participate in much needed clinical research. Opponents believe that current law provides sufficient protection. They are primarily concerned that new legislation will provide further incentives and additional opportunities for litigation against employers.

* Excerpted from CRS Report RL33903, dated March 7, 2007.

Collectively, genetic diseases and common diseases with a genetic component pose a significant public health burden. With completion of the human genome sequence, scientists are now focusing on the development of clinical applications based on the sequence information. One such application, clinical genetic testing, is becoming available at a rapid rate, and some tests are beginning to be included in health insurance benefits packages. Genetic testing may both facilitate and be inhibited by the potential for genetic discrimination. Issues surrounding nondiscrimination addressed in this report include:

- What is health information and how is it currently used by health insurers and employers?
- What is genetic information?
- Is genetic information different from other health information?
- What evidence exists to suggest that discrimination is a problem?
- Would the proposed legislation be sufficient to protect "genetic information" and "genetic tests" that are of concern?

INTRODUCTION

In order for Congress to address the key issue that it faces with respect to genetic discrimination, namely, whether the potential for genetic discrimination by employers and insurers merits protections for genetic information that are more extensive than those already in place for health information in general, there are several fundamental points that it may wish to consider. These include an understanding of what genetic information and discrimination are, how current laws affect employers' and insurers' use of genetic and other health information, how proposed legislation would amend current law, and the arguments that have been made both in favor of and against the passage of legislation.

Properly defining genetic information in potential nondiscrimination legislation is essential, as the scope of the definition will largely determine the types of activities that are permitted and proscribed. Yet this basic concept may prove to be complex, as many types of health information have a genetic component. Genetic information may be defined and derived in a number of ways. Of course, it may be obtained via genetic testing. However, it may also be discernable through other laboratory testing that does not involve a specific examination of genes, such as some protein or molecular testing. It may sometimes be derived through physical examination (for example, Down's syndrome, which has a genetic basis, has specific physical characteristics such as a single crease across each palm). Finally, genetic information may be discernable from a family's medical history, which might reveal risks for certain types of cancer, hypertension, and a myriad of other diseases with a genetic component.

Once the definition of genetic information is settled, the question of what constitutes discrimination based on that information can be addressed. In the context of the current debate in Congress, genetic discrimination can be defined as the potential use of an individual's genetic information by employers or health insurers to discriminate against that individual in employment decisions (hiring, promotions, firing) or health insurance coverage decisions (eligibility or premiums). Although the use of health information, including genetic information, by employers and insurers is currently regulated, some argue that genetic information merits special protections under the law.

Three federal laws and a presidential order touch on the issues raised by the use of genetic information: the Americans with Disabilities Act (ADA); Title VII of the Civil Rights Act of 1963; the Health Insurance Portability and Accountability Act (HIPAA); and Executive Order 13145, *To Prohibit Discrimination in Federal Employment Based on Genetic Information* (65 FR 6877).[1] The ADA protects people from discrimination based on existing disability, history of disability, and perception of disability in employment. The executive order prohibits discrimination against federal employees based on protected genetic information, or information about a request for or the receipt of genetic services.

In general, the HIPAA statute limits denial of coverage based on pre-existing conditions to 12 months. In the absence of a current diagnosis, the HIPAA statute would not consider predictions of risk of future disease based on genetic information to be a pre-existing condition. In addition, the health information privacy rule, issued in 2000 pursuant to HIPAA's Administrative Simplification provisions, restricts the disclosure of health information, including genetic information, by group and individual health plans. The HIPAA privacy rule also allows group and individual health plans to use some health information (which could include genetic information) in underwriting. The Civil Rights Act provides some protections against genetic discrimination against members of a protected group, such as persons of a certain race, color, religion, sex or national origin.[2]

The existence and scope of state anti-discrimination legislation that could be interpreted to cover genetics varies.[3] Most state laws prohibit: (i) discrimination based on particular traits or diseases; (ii) discrimination based on genetic test results; or (iii) insurers or employers from requiring that an individual take a genetic test and using the results.[4]

Legislation reintroduced in the 110th Congress (S. 358 / H.R. 493) has been marked up by the House Committee on Education and Labor and the Senate Committee on Health, Education, Labor and Pensions. The legislation would extend current federal protections against discrimination to health insurers in the individual market, and would further limit the use and disclosure of genetic information. The bills would also bar insurers from using genetic information or family history of disease in underwriting for an individual (as an individual or applied to a group).[5]

S. 358 and H.R. 493 would also prohibit discrimination in employment because of genetic information and, with certain exceptions, prohibit an employer from requesting, requiring, or purchasing genetic information. If such information were obtained, the bills would require that it be treated as part of a confidential medical record. The bills include detailed provisions on enforcement which generally apply the remedies available in existing civil rights laws such as Title VII of the Civil Rights Act of 1964 (42 U.S.C. § 2000e-4 et seq). Neither bill addresses life or disability insurance.

Genetic nondiscrimination legislation has been debated since the 103rd Congress.[6] Since that time, many of the arguments and positions supporting and opposing genetic nondiscrimination legislation have remained largely unchanged. On January 18, 2007, President Bush called on Congress to pass bipartisan genetic nondiscrimination legislation.[7] Genetic nondiscrimination legislation is supported by consumer groups, the medical profession, researchers and the medical products industry (including pharmaceutical companies). Opposition to genetic nondiscrimination legislation has come from some members of the insurance industry and from employers, represented broadly by the Genetic

Information Nondiscrimination in Employment (GINE) Coalition,[8] which includes the U.S. Chamber of Commerce.

Supporters of the legislation argue that current laws are not clear on protection from discrimination based on genetic information; because existing federal laws have not been tested in court, the extent of their protection of genetic information is not assured. Despite the fact that few cases of genetic discrimination can be documented, supporters argue that proper protections are necessary to allay the fears of individuals about the potential for discriminatory practices. Allaying the public's fears, they argue, will encourage individuals to seek beneficial health services, participate in much-needed clinical research, .and otherwise reap the benefits of the publicly funded Human Genome Project (HGP).

Many professional and consumer groups argue that individuals should not be penalized in their ability to obtain insurance or a job because medical science can identify a genetic condition or a gene that predisposes a person to a future illness, but cannot yet offer an effective treatment. For example, the American Civil Liberties Union (ACLU) stated at a hearing in 2001 that "Americans should be judged on their actual abilities, not their potential disabilities."[9] On the other hand, this may create a disparity between people whose medical conditions have treatments available and those whose do not.

Opponents of enacting special legislation to prevent potential discrimination on the basis of genetic information argue that current federal and state protections are sufficient. The insurance industry also argues that additional regulation would be confusing, unnecessary and costly. They claim that it would be unfair to prohibit them from acquiring genetic information when they already use other health information. Some groups, such as the American Association of Health Plans (now a part of the America's Health Insurance Plans), support the premise of federal nondiscrimination legislation and have indicated support for legislation that is consistent with their principles.[10] However, others would further limit the definition of genetic information.[11] One bill introduced in the 108th Congress (H.R. 3636) would have prohibited health insurers from discriminating based on predictive genetic information but would not have affected employers. The bill had no cosponsors, and many consumer groups indicated that they would not support nondiscrimination legislation without both insurance and employment provisions.

Some employers question whether legislation is necessary because there are few documented cases of discrimination based on genetic information, and there is no evidence that employers would use the information if they had it. In addition, employers argue that existing law provides adequate protection against genetic discrimination in employment. Randy Johnson, vice president of the U.S. Chamber of Commerce's office of labor policy, stated that if the legislation were to pass, it should be narrowed to acknowledge that employers should be able to make employment decisions based on information that some workers with specified genetic markers could pose a "significant risk to others."[12] Other business coalition members suggest that the definition of "family member" should be revised to include only immediate family. Many also support federal preemption whereby any new federal law would preempt existing state law in this area.

This report provides an overview of the scope and current permissible uses of health information and genetic information. It reviews the existing evidence of genetic discrimination and the impact of the fear of discrimination. Then it provides a more detailed discussion of S. 358/H.R. 493 and the key issues raised by the genetic nondiscrimination bills.

For a more detailed discussion of genetic testing and public policy, see CRS Report RL33832, *Genetic Testing: Scientific Background for Policymakers*, by Amanda K. Sarata.

HEALTH INFORMATION

Understanding how health information is currently used and regulated provides a framework for discussion about whether extra protections are necessary for genetic information, and if so, which protections are most appropriate. Health information, which includes genetic information, is currently used by health insurers and employers. It is often presumed confidential, but increasing capabilities to store and rapidly transfer data electronically escalate the challenge of protecting privacy. Both the ways in which health insurers and employers use and are restricted from using health information are discussed in the sections that follow.

Use of Genetic and Other Health Information by Health Insurers

Several federal laws help provide some protection against genetic discrimination in health insurance. These laws include the Health Insurance Portability and Accountability Act (HIPAA) of 1996 (specifically Title I: Health Care Access, Portability, and Renewability); the Social Security Act (SSA); and the HIPAA privacy rule. HIPAA prohibits group health plans from imposing a preexisting condition exclusion on the basis of genetic information or establishing eligibility requirements for any individual based on genetic information. However, HIPAA does not prohibit a group health plan from charging all members of a group higher premiums on the basis of an individual's genetic information. The SSA contains provisions that prohibit discrimination in the pricing or issuance of Medigap policies on the basis of health status, but it does not specifically state that health status includes genetic information.

The privacy rule gives patients the right of access to their medical information and places certain limitations on when and how health plans and health care providers may use and disclose medical information. Generally, plans may use and disclose information for their own treatment, payment, and health care operations without the individual's authorization and with few restrictions. The rule covers all individually identifiable health information, including genetic tests and information about an individual's family history. The rule permits a group health plan to disclose individually identifiable health information to an employer that sponsors the plan, provided the information is used only for plan administration purposes.

Health insurers typically use family history, among many health factors, in the process of placing individuals or groups in a risk category for determining their premiums (underwriting). Individuals or groups at higher risk may be charged higher premiums to cover the anticipated costs of their care. Traditional approaches to underwriting also use age, sex, type of occupation, financial stability of group members, employee turnover and prior cost (of care) experience to determine what a group's insurance premium should be.

In general, premiums for a large group with one or two sick members can remain relatively stable, as the cost of the sick individuals is spread among all members of the group.

However, as groups become smaller, the cost of insurance for the group is more dependent on the health of the individual group members, since one sick individual in a small group can result in high premiums for the whole group. Individuals who are not part of a group coverage, seeking to purchase individual health insurance, must bear the entire premium increase associated with any illness, thus making such insurance prohibitively expensive for many sick individuals.

Insurers claim that most genetic information is not currently useful to the underwriting process because the clinical significance and relationship to the severity of illness is not known for many conditions. However, once the link to future illness is established and the costs thereof become predictable, insurers' use of genetic information might be no different than the use of other diagnostic information. Some actuaries agree that adding diagnostic information significantly improves the power of traditional underwriting methods to predict future medical expense.[13]

One author has provided a model demonstrating how genetic information (including family history) that has a known correlation to a specific disease, such as Huntington's disease or breast cancer, could be used to underwrite life insurance.[14] Some health care providers and consumers fear that the model could also be applied to health insurance. The model's author suggests that insurers support screening for genetic mutations for which preventive interventions can reduce the risk of death. However, health insurers may disagree, depending on the nature, expense and effectiveness of the interventions in preventing symptoms and other medical costs of treating an acute or chronic illness. That which reduces the risk of death may not reduce health or disability expenses (and lower life insurance premiums). In addition, health insurers may be reluctant to bear the costs of preventive care. Particularly in a climate in which individuals change health insurers frequently, an insurer that pays for prevention may not ultimately reap the financial benefits of avoiding the illness.

The Problem of Adverse Selection

The predictive power of genetic testing raises a concern for insurers about the possibility of adverse selection. Adverse selection can occur when an insurance applicant knows — and the insurance company does not know — that the applicant has some health risk, possibly due to genetic information. In this case, the applicant may be motivated to purchase insurance with greater coverage and may be able to do so at a lesser premium.

Some argue that the specter of adverse selection requires that insurance companies have access to genetic information, or else their financial solvency may be threatened because individuals might obtain insurance at premiums that did not accurately reflect their risk of expenditures.[15] Others argue that concerns about adverse selection with respect to genetic information may be unfounded. The majority of Americans receive their insurance through their employers, which are group rated (i.e., premiums are based on an assessment of the average risk among all employees). This system creates incentives for low-risk individuals to purchase coverage, thus diminishing the potential impact of adverse selection. In addition, some note that genetic information about disease risk may prove to be so complicated as to be essentially useless to an insurer.[16] For example, for a complex multigenic disease, there may be numerous genes involved, each of which contributes relatively little to an individual's risk of developing disease. In addition, these variants will be modified by environmental factors that further complicate the analysis.

Use of Genetic and Other Health Information by Employers

One federal law, the Americans with Disabilities Act (ADA), may provide some protections against employers' use of employees' genetic information. The ADA prohibits employers from revoking an offer, or from making other promotion decisions on the basis of that health information. Though genetics is not specifically addressed by the ADA, the Equal Employment Opportunities Commission (EEOC) interprets the ADA to mean that employees and/or job applicants cannot be required to undergo genetic screening. However, current law permits employers to require medical examinations of prospective employees who have been given conditional offers of employment, if all employees in a similar situation are given the medical exam. Employers may also receive information related to applicants' or employees' current disability or health status when the information is related to the individuals' abilities to do their job.[17]

Supporters of genetic nondiscrimination legislation argue that because ADA does not explicitly address genetics, the ADA protections that would be applied by the court system are not clear.[18] Opponents argue that the ADA protections are sufficient, and that the proposed legislation is not clear on workplace situations where an employee's genetic makeup could interfere with the major functions of the individual's job or put others at risk of harm.

Another federal law, the Occupational Safety and Hazard Act (OSHA), may permit employers to conduct some genetic tests on employees. OSHA establishes a legal duty for employers to protect employees from hazards in the workplace. Although the statute does not require an employer to perform particular tests, the employer may choose to implement programs that monitor employees' potential exposure to toxic or hazardous elements. Standards for these programs allow for genetic testing.[19]

Genetic monitoring for acquired damage resulting from exposure to a toxic element is different from genetic screening for an inherited predisposition to an occupationally related disease.[20] For example, monitoring may be used to determine if an employee is developing DNA damage from being exposed to asbestos. On the other hand, a different type of test could potentially determine if the employee were more susceptible to asbestos damage to begin with. The distinction may be relevant should questions arise regarding whether any ill-health effects sustained by the worker were a result of occupational exposure.

Genetic Information

As noted in the introduction, the definition of genetic information is a key issue for Congress in its consideration of genetic nondiscrimination legislation, because the broader the definition the more expansive the prohibitions on discrimination. The definition of genetic information varies among sources. Genetic information is generally described as the information from a genetic test about genes, gene products, inherited characteristics or other traits that are derived from an individual or an individual's family member(s). Information about an individual's current health status (such as sex, age, results of physical examination, and chemical, blood, or urine analysis, where the analyses do not provide information about an individual's genotype) is generally not considered to be genetic information. The two key sources of genetic information are family medical histories and genetic test results.

Is Genetic Information Different from Other Health Information?

Understanding the ways in which genetic information is like and unlike other types of information can help to inform the debate over the need for genetic-specific nondiscrimination legislation. Congress faces two questions on this topic. First, is genetic information different from other health information? Second, if so, do the differences indicate that genetic information merits additional protections?

Genetic information has been described as being different from other health information because of factors such as its stability, its unique predictive qualities, its potential use for individual and familial identification, and the impact that public fear of discrimination is having on the behavior of patients and healthcare providers. Some argue that these factors may make the misuse of genetic information particularly detrimental to individuals, and, therefore, that the information deserves special protections. Further, they argue that the public health benefits that could come from large-scale genetic research and the utilization of new genetic technologies may not be fully realized unless public fear is assuaged by genetic nondiscrimination legislation.

Those opposed to special protections assert that genetic information is fundamentally no different than other health data, at least not in ways relevant to special protections, and that genetic information is already adequately protected by medical privacy laws. The Senate report for S. 1053 (S.Rept. 108-122), the genetic nondiscrimination bill that was passed by the Senate in 2003, included the statement that eventually "it may not be possible or even desirable in health care delivery or scientific research to isolate genetic information as it pervades health information."

To address the question of whether genetic information merits special protections, one study compared the experiences, attitudes and beliefs of persons with genetic conditions (cystic fibrosis and sickle cell disease) to those with other serious medical conditions (diabetes, HIV, breast cancer and colon cancer) and to persons at risk for developing a disease (breast or colon cancer) due to strong family history. The authors found that in most instances, patients felt strongly that their health information needed to be protected regardless of whether it was genetic. In fact, respondents indicated that information about non-genetic stigmatizing conditions — such as abortion history, mental health history, drug and alcohol history, HIV status, and sexually transmitted disease — needed special protection. Based on their findings, the authors concluded that separate privacy policies for genetic and non-genetic health information would be unwarranted.[21]

Other studies and public opinion polls suggest that patients and members of the community desire and may benefit from additional protections for their genetic information.[22] A 2003 study of 470 people with a family history of colorectal cancer showed that nearly half rated their level of concern about genetic discrimination as high. Those individuals with high levels of concern indicated that they would be significantly less likely to consider meeting with a health care professional to discuss genetic testing, or to undergo testing. A 2004 survey by the Center for Genetics and Public Policy found that 92% of survey respondents thought employers should not have access to their genetic test results, and 80% opposed letting insurance companies have access to results.

WHAT EVIDENCE IS THERE THAT GENETIC DISCRIMINATION EXISTS?

Critics of genetic nondiscrimination legislation have argued that legislation is not necessary because genetic discrimination is not occurring. There have indeed been relatively few reported cases of genetic discrimination in health insurance and employment. Rothenberg and Terry hypothesize that this is because: (1) the use of genetic information by employers and insurers is not widespread; (2) affected persons may not know the underlying basis for adverse employment or insurance decisions; and (3) many cases may go unreported because of disincentives associated with publicizing discrimination lawsuits.[23] Reports of cases of genetic discrimination and genetic testing by employers are presented below.

Cases of Genetic Discrimination

There have been a few studies of the prevalence of genetic discrimination in health insurance, employment, and other settings, and these studies are quite dated. One study reported that 22% of survey respondents indicated that they or a family member were refused health insurance as a result of a genetic condition.[24] This study was strongly criticized by the Health Insurance Association of America (HIAA) at the time, which argued that there is no evidence showing that insurers engage in genetic discrimination, and that federal legislation to prohibit discrimination based on genetic information is unnecessary.[25] However, another study found that a number of institutions, including health and life insurance companies, health care providers, blood banks, adoption agencies, the military and schools, were reported to have engaged in genetic discrimination against asymptomatic individuals. The alleged discriminatory practices included an insurance company treating a genetic diagnosis as a preexisting condition, an adoption agency refusing to allow a woman at risk for Huntington's disease to adopt a child, and an employer terminating an employee after the employee disclosed a risk of Huntington's disease.[26]

On October 18, 2004, several individuals shared stories of genetic discrimination with the Secretary's Advisory Committee on Genetics, Health and Society (SACGHS).[27] These cases are highlighted below:

- Phil Hardt has hemophilia B, a bleeding disorder, and Huntington's disease. He testified that a human resource manager for an early employer had indicated that he should withhold information about his hemophilia and any bleeding episodes from his employer or he would never be promoted or trained. In addition, he indicated that his daughter was unable to receive mortgage life insurance unless she tested negative for Huntington's disease. His grandson was denied health insurance because of the hemophilia B that he inherited, and he was forced to accept lower wages so that they could qualify for state welfare and insurance coverage. Two of his other children decided to pay out of pocket to be tested anonymously for Huntington's disease to protect them from discrimination. Mr. Hardt applied — and was rejected — for long-term care insurance.

- Rebecca Fisher, a mother and early-onset breast cancer survivor with a strong family history recounted how her employer, a small, self-insured community hospital, was more concerned that the cost of her bone marrow transplantation and other health care had exceeded the cap for that year than with her health or productivity.
- Tonia Phillips, a woman with a BRCA1 mutation in her family, chose to undergo prophylactic surgery to reduce her risk of breast and/or ovarian cancer. After her procedures, her employer-sponsored health insurance policy had increased by $13,000. Her employer asked her to switch to her husband's policy, and in doing so, indicated that she would receive a wage increase.
- Paula Funk, another individual who carried a BRCA1 mutation, indicated that, because of the potential for discrimination, she and her family paid out of pocket for testing so her physicians and health care providers would not write her BRCA1 status on insurance claims forms. She further testified regarding her difficulty in finding an insurance company that would cover herself and her husband, co-owners of a small business, as a group so that their premiums would be affordable, given her family history and genetic testing status.
- Heidi Williams, an individual diagnosed with alpha-1 antitrypsin deficiency,[28] also spoke at a press conference at the House of Representatives on April 1, 2004. She explained that a large health insurance company (Humana) had denied health insurance coverage for her two children on the basis that they were carriers of alpha-1 antitrypsin disease. Carriers only have one copy of an abnormal gene, and typically do not exhibit symptoms of the disease. After receiving inquiries from the Genetic Alliance (a consumer advocacy organization) and the press, the insurance company reversed its decision to deny coverage, and provided six months of free coverage.
- On July 20, 2000, Terri Seargent, also an individual diagnosed with alpha-1 antitrypsin deficiency, filed a statement with the Senate Health, Education, Labor and Pension Committee indicating that soon after her diagnosis, she was unexpectedly released from employment. Without a job, and having a pre-existing condition, she also lost her health, life and disability insurance. Later, an investigation by the Equal Employment Opportunity Commission (EEOC) supported her allegation of discrimination under the Americans with Disabilities Act (ADA).[29]

It is difficult to gauge the appropriate weight that clusters of stories like those above should have in the policy arena. On one hand, drawing broad conclusions based on a few examples may not be valid. On the other hand, obtaining information from a representative sample of the population may be difficult, because individuals may be reluctant to share their personal genetic information.

Genetic Testing by Employers

Employers' testing of employees for genetic markers is not currently believed to be a widespread practice; however, surveys of employer practice and employee experience indicate that some instances exist. No cases of employment discrimination based on genetics have been decided in a federal court or the U.S. Supreme Court.

However, several have been brought or threatened, and two cases were settled out of court.[30]

Surveys of Employers

Employers have long been interested in identifying "optimal" employees using non-health characteristics — such as behavior (i.e., substance abuse, mental instability, compulsive disorders) or intelligence — to identify special skills or deficits that are predictive of productivity.[31] Though behavioral genetic testing is not ready for commercial use (largely due to the very complex interaction of genes and the environment), other forms of testing are common.

The American Management Association (AMA) has conducted several surveys of employers' medical testing practices. In a1998 survey,[32] the AMA questioned the employers about their use and understanding of what constituted a genetic test. Respondents were presented with National Institutes of Health's definition of genetic test: "an analysis of human DNA, RNA, chromosomes, proteins, and certain metabolites in order to detect heritable disease-related genotypes, mutations, phenotypes, or karyotypes for clinical purposes. Such purposes include predicting risk of disease, identifying carriers, and establishing prenatal and clinical diagnosis or prognosis." Only two respondents (out of 1,627) indicated that they performed genetic testing. A larger percentage (14.3%) indicated testing for "susceptibility to workplace hazards." The results were modified by a 1999 follow-up survey in which AMA found that not all of the testing their 1998 respondents had characterized as "genetic" actually was.[33] Only nine of 44 employers who indicated having testing programs actually had genetic testing programs. Some employers believed that any blood test constituted genetic testing; others believed that diagnostic testing, rather than susceptibility testing, was genetic testing.

In 2001, the AMA conducted another survey of employers' medical testing practices.[34] The results indicated that 68% of major U.S. firms required medical examinations for new hires, current employees, or both. These were most frequently required in public administration and manufacturing positions and less frequently in business or professional positions. Establishing "fitness for duty" was the leading reason that firms engaged in complete medical examinations (48% of respondents). Testing for illegal substance use was the most common form of workplace testing, practiced by 67% of employers. Some employers also reported testing new or current employees for the genetic diseases sickle cell anemia (1.3%) or Huntington's disease (0.4%), and a larger proportion asked about family medical history (20.1%). In addition, some employers indicated that they used the medical test results — about sickle cell anemia (1.0%), about Huntington's disease (0.8%), and about family history (5.5%) — for purposes of hiring, reassigning, retaining or dismissing employees.

Surveys of Consumers

A 1996 study of 332 consumers who were members of genetic support groups found that 13% of respondents reported that they or another family member were denied a job or let go because of a genetic condition in the family.[35] The experience was significantly different for respondents who had a genetic condition (21%) compared to respondents who did not have a genetic condition (4%). Two examples were highlighted: one respondent, a man with a sex chromosome disorder, indicated that he was denied a job when a doctor wrote the name of the disorder on his medical report during his pre-employment physical. The potential employer told the applicant of the decision and, knowing it was illegal, also stated that they would deny having the conversation. In the second example, a woman with a skeletal disorder reported that her employment was terminated after she informed her employer of her diagnosis. The woman sought legal counsel, and the termination was withdrawn.

Authors of a recently published study interviewed approximately 100 adults or parents of children with sickle cell disease, cystic fibrosis, diabetes, and HIV, and 200 adults with or at risk for breast or colon cancer about their experiences and attitudes regarding health insurance.[36] Twenty-seven percent of the respondents self-reported having been denied health insurance or offered insurance at a prohibitively expensive rate. Respondents with sickle cell disease and cystic fibrosis were twice as likely to report this as those with non-genetic conditions (e.g., HIV). More than one-third of all respondents thought there was a high chance they would be denied health insurance in the future or their insurance would become unaffordable. While the study may have suggested that insurers make decisions based on genetic information or diseases, S. 358 / H.R. 493 would only limit discrimination due to genetic predisposition to diseases. The bills would have no effect on insurance availability or costs for people like many of those in the study who had manifested genetic diseases.

Court Cases and Legal Settlements

To date, there have been two court cases alleging genetic discrimination. In 2002, Burlington Northern Santa Fe Railway Corporation, one of the country's biggest railroads, agreed to pay $2.2 million to settle charges related to genetic testing and discrimination. Employees charged those who had filed for workers compensation for carpel tunnel syndrome (CTS) were tested without their knowledge for a genetic marker dubiously associated with the syndrome. CTS is a painful hand and wrist condition caused by repetitive motion. The railway denied violating the law, and insisted that testing was necessary to determine the cause of injury to 36 employees who claimed to have job-related CTS (20 actually underwent testing before the program was voluntarily suspended). Burlington Northern halted the testing under the terms of a settlement shortly after a lawsuit was filed.[37]

In another case, Lawrence Berkeley Laboratory was accused of conducting pre-employment screening for sensitive medical information, testing for genetic traits such as sickle cell trait, and for non-genetic factors such as syphilis and pregnancy.[38] The case was settled out of court in 1999. Prior to settlement, the employees had filed a court case, claiming that the Laboratory had violated Title VII and right to privacy as guaranteed in the U.S. and California Constitutions. In response, the laboratory sought to have the case dismissed without a trial (in summary judgement), claiming that the employees had waited so long after the alleged testing to file their case that their right to sue had expired (the statue of limitations had tolled). On this issue, an appellate court sided with the plaintiffs, determining that the question of when employees knew or had reason to know that the laboratory was conducting testing should be decided by a court (issues of material fact existed), thus precluding summary judgement. (*Norman-Bloodsaw v. Lawrence Berkeley Laboratory* (135 F.3d 1260, 1269; 9th Cir. 1998)).

IMPACT OF THE FEAR OF DISCRIMINATION ON BEHAVIOR

While there are few documented cases of genetic discrimination by employers and health insurers, studies have shown that public fear of discrimination influences both the use of genetic testing and the use of genetic information by consumers and health professionals. Fear of genetic discrimination may cause consumers to refuse genetic testing and therapies that could be beneficial to their health. It may deter people from participating in genetic research, thus slowing the development of new technologies. In other words, whether or not genetic discrimination is actually occurring, public worry about the issue may itself have detrimental effects. Related questions have been raised about whether genetic counseling, in which professionals inform and assist patients making genetic-related healthcare decisions, may serve to unduly increase the fear of discrimination, amplifying the behavioral impact. Both examples of the behavioral impact of genetic discrimination and investigation into the role of genetic counseling are presented in this section.

Examples of the Impact of Fear of Discrimination on Behavior

In January 2000, the Secretary's Advisory Committee on Genetic Testing (SACGT) sponsored a public forum that focused on the impact that the fear of genetic discrimination was having on various groups. SACGT received comments from patients, consumers, health professionals, scientists, genetic test developers, educators, industry representatives, policymakers, lawyers, students and others representing a wide range of diverse ethnic and racial groups, and from a survey mailed to 2,500 individuals.[39] The comments revealed several anecdotal cases of discrimination, and resulted in the committee forwarding two letters to the Secretary of Health and Human Services (HHS) urging support for nondiscrimination protections:

> During consultations with the public SACGT heard from many Americans who are concerned about the misuse of genetic information by third parties, such as health insurers and employers, and the potential for discrimination based on that information. Many stated that fear of genetic discrimination would dissuade them from undergoing a genetic test or participating in genetic research studies. Others stated that they would pay out of pocket for a genetic test to prevent the results from being placed in their medical record. Such concerns are a deterrent to advances in the field of genetic testing and may limit the realization of the benefits of genetic testing.[40]

Some examples of the specific impact that the fear of genetic discrimination has on behavior were provided in October 2004, when several individuals testified at a SACGHS meeting:[41]

- Carolina Hinestrosa, a 10-year, two-time survivor of breast cancer and executive vice president for programs and planning of the National Breast Cancer Coalition stated that despite her strong personal and family history, she has not undergone genetic testing for fear of discrimination against herself and her daughter.
- A mother, Phaedra Malatek, described how her family has not taken advantage of the health benefits of genetic testing for hemochromatosis that ran in her family because of their fear of losing their health insurance, and possible discrimination against her children when they seek employment.

Surveys of professionals and patients suggest that individuals are most likely to withhold information about genetic testing from insurance companies and their employers. A survey of genetic counselors[42] found that, should counselors themselves be at risk of developing either breast cancer or hereditary non-polyposis colon cancer, most (108 out of 159 surveyed) would not submit charges to their insurance companies primarily because of the fear of discrimination. Twenty-five percent would use an alias when obtaining a test to reduce the risk of discrimination and maximize confidentiality. Most respondents indicated that, while they would share results with their physicians, family and friends, 60% would not share the information with colleagues because of the need for privacy and fear of job discrimination based on the result.[43]

Of 91 participants in a study on hereditary pancreatitis, 22% believed that knowing their test results “might lead to medical insurance discrimination” for themselves or their families. While most individuals would share information with a physician or their family, only 4% indicated they would share results with their insurance companies, and 20% would share them with their employers.[44] Another study of 98 extended families with a history of breast or ovarian cancer, reported on 716 of 1,315 individuals who underwent counseling and DNA testing. Before receiving results, about half were concerned about insurance discrimination, and 1% indicated that they felt strongly that their family history of cancer had been the basis for insurance discrimination.[45]

A group of scientists at the University of Michigan offered genetic testing for susceptibility to breast cancer to 184 individuals participating in a cancer risk evaluation clinic. Patients were charged about $225 for the initial consultation, and were required to pay Myriad Genetics directly for any testing they pursued. At the time, Myriad charged $395 for analysis of a single mutation, $450 for analysis of three common mutations found in individuals of Ashkenazi Jewish descent, and $2,400 for full sequencing of the breast cancer susceptibility genes (also called BRCA1 and 2). Patients had the option of self-paying, or billing their insurance companies. Though discussion of potential discrimination was standard practice in the counseling session that accompanied testing, the researchers only counted concerns initiated by the patient during the session. Of the 184 patients, 106 underwent testing. Of the 78 patients who declined testing, 48 (or 26% of the original cohort of 184) declined due to concerns about cost, confidentiality or insurance discrimination.[46] The authors found it difficult to separate these concerns. Although a patient may have wanted to self-pay for fear of potential discrimination, the high cost of testing may have forced the patient to choose to bill insurance, or decline testing. The authors estimated that approximately 14% of patients eligible for testing would have had a BRCA mutation, but would not undergo testing because of cost, discrimination, or confidentiality concerns.

A follow-up telephone interview was conducted with 92 of the 184 patients concerning their actual experiences with their insurance companies. Of the 92, 15% paid out of pocket, intentionally not involving their insurance companies, while 38% (35 of 92) indicated that they did not have any problems obtaining insurance coverage for the services requested. However, of those 35 patients, 23 only requested payment for the consult and surgery — not the testing — from their insurers. The remaining 47% experienced various difficulties in obtaining coverage for some or all of the services. The patient's family income was a significant factor in the decision to seek insurance reimbursement. In another study of 68 patients offered genetic testing for breast cancer, while 18 had access to free testing, and 13 sought insurance reimbursement, the remaining 37 chose to pay out of pocket citing concerns over insurability and confidentiality reasons.[47] Other authors have postulated that those with the lowest income who were covered by government healthcare programs, such as Medicaid, may be less concerned about genetic discrimination because their eligibility for health insurance does not depend on health status or underwriting decisions.[48]

The Role of Genetic Counseling

When viewing evidence of the ways in which fear of genetic discrimination affects behavior, some have questioned whether genetic counseling itself may inadvertently add to the fear. The risk of discrimination by employers and insurers is often discussed in the counseling session that accompanies testing. Most counselors typically spend up to 15 minutes of a one- to two-hour counseling session discussing patient concerns about discrimination, even in states with more comprehensive anti-discrimination laws. Counselors typically note that actual cases of discrimination are few, and will provide information regarding the various legal protections.[49] While many counselors indicate that a significant proportion (25-50%) of patients may decline testing due to potential discrimination, other patients accept testing because the benefits of the information to their health or the health of a relative outweigh the risk of discrimination. Either way, counselors note that the potential risk adds to an already stressful situation.

In order to reassure patients about privacy, genetic counselors may vary their practices in several ways: they may be discreet about how a visit is documented (i.e., for cancer screening, not genetic testing); they may not send the results to the referring physician unless asked specifically by the patient to do so; or, they may request that the physician keep the results in a separate medical record. Some will forward coded samples to the laboratories for testing. Many genetic counselors will themselves maintain patient files that are separate from the rest of the hospital or medical center's records to minimize the possibility that an insurer will obtain genetic information in the process of reviewing a medical record for reimbursement.[50]

Genetic counselors note that the fears associated with predictive testing for future adult onset illness are not as apparent in testing in the prenatal and pediatric populations. Presumably this is because of the "crisis atmosphere" created with the diagnosis of a potential birth defect and the parents' decision of whether or not to terminate a pregnancy. In some cases including those involving newborns, the fear of insurability may be mitigated by the fact that children are covered under their parents' policies. However, some counselors have expressed concern about the way in which genetic information will be viewed when children become adults and have to find insurance on their own.[51]

The Genetic Information Nondiscrimination Act of 2007 (S. 358/H.R. 493)

The Genetic Information Nondiscrimination Act of 2007 would restrict insurers' and employers' acquisition and use of genetic information in several ways. These restrictions build upon those already imposed in current law. The specifics of the proposed restrictions have sparked debates in both the employment and insurance arenas since they were first proposed. This section of the report summarizes the current privacy protections in place for both insurers and employers, and then surveys the persistent debates that have accompanied genetic nondiscrimination legislation generally.

Title I: Genetic Nondiscrimination and Health Insurance

Title 1 of S. 358 and H.R. 493 would extend the current HIPAA protections against discrimination by group health plans and issuers of health insurance in both the group and individual markets, and restrict their acquisition, use and disclosure of genetic information. Currently, group plans and insurance issuers may require individuals to provide genetic information or undergo genetic tests as a condition of issuing coverage. The HIPAA privacy rule permits plans and insurers to use and disclose genetic information for health care operations, a broadly defined term that includes underwriting, premium rating, and other activities related to the creation, renewal, or replacement of an insurance contract.

Under HIPAA's current group market protections against discrimination, plans or insurance issuers may not: (1) deny enrollment to an individual enrolling as part of a group based on the individual's health status, which is defined to include genetic information; or (2) charge individuals enrolling as part of a group more than others in the group based on genetic information. However, insurers may charge the entire group more based on genetic information about an individual or individuals within the group. In the individual market, HIPAA permits insurers to set premiums based on an applicant's genetic information, or deny that applicant coverage if the individual is not HIPAA-protected (although some states prohibit such activity).[52]

The bills would place the following restrictions on group health plans and health insurers.

Genetic Testing Requirements Prohibited

The bills would prohibit group plans and insurers from requesting or requiring that individuals or their family members undergo a genetic test. However, they would not limit the ability of a health care professional to provide health services even if they were employed by or affiliated with a group health plan or health insurance issuer. That is, health care professionals who are providing care may request or suggest that individuals or their family undergo a test.

Use and Disclosure of Genetic Information Restricted

The bills would prohibit group plans and insurers from requesting, requiring, purchasing, using or disclosing genetic information for the purposes of underwriting, eligibility determination (before or during the enrollment process), premium rating, or the creation, renewal, or replacement of a health insurance plan or contract. "Incidental collection" of genetic information would not be considered a violation.

Health Insurance Discrimination Disallowed

The bills would prohibit plans and insurers in the group health insurance market from: (1) denying enrollment to an individual based on genetic information about that individual or their family members (as noted above, a similar nondiscrimination provision is already in HIPAA); and (2) adjusting a group's premium based on genetic information about an individual in the group or their family members. In the individual market, the bills would prohibit insurers from denying enrollment or adjusting premiums based on genetic information about the individual or their family members.

Penalties for Violations Permitted

The bills would permit the Secretary to impose a penalty of $100 per day during a period of noncompliance with the provisions in Title I. Where willful neglect was found, they would establish a minimum penalty of $2,500, or $15,000 for more severe or prolonged violations.

Title II: Genetic Nondiscrimination and Employment

Title II of S. 358 and H.R. 493 would make it unlawful employment practice for an employer to discriminate against an employee on the basis of genetic information. Employers also would be prohibited from acquiring genetic information, except under certain specified circumstances (see below). The bills would cover employers and employees as defined in Sections 701 and 717 of the Civil Rights Act of 1964, state employees and employers described in the Government Employee Rights Act of 1991, employees and employers described in the Congressional Accountability Act of 1995 and as defined in Section 3 U.S.C. 411(c), and job applicants. The bills would place the following restrictions on employers.

Genetic Testing Requirements Prohibited

The bills would prohibit employers, employment agencies and labor organizations from requiring or requesting that an individual or a family member undergo a genetic test. However, they would not limit the ability of a health care professional to provide health services; that is, health care professionals who are providing care could request or suggest that individuals or their family members undergo testing in the context of providing care.

Discrimination in Employment Practices Disallowed

The bills would prohibit employers, employment agencies, and labor organizations from using genetic information when making decisions about employees' or applicants' hiring, promotion, or eligibility or selection for training programs or apprenticeships.

Acquisition of Genetic Information Restricted

Generally, the bills would prohibit employers, employment agencies, and labor organizations from requesting, requiring or purchasing genetic information. They would allow employers, employment agencies and labor organizations to acquire genetic information about an individual in the following circumstances:

- when they offered a health service program;
- when the employee provided written authorization;
- when the information was used to monitor the biological effects of toxic substances in the workplace, but only if:

  — the genetic monitoring was required by federal or state law;
  — the employee provided written authorization;
  — the employer provided written notice of genetic monitoring;
  — the employee was informed of the monitoring results;
  — the monitoring was conducted in compliance with federal genetic monitoring regulations; and
  — the identity of specific employees was not disclosed.

In addition, the proposed bills would allow an employer to obtain genetic information in the following situations:

- when the employer inadvertently requested or required family medical history;
- when the employer offered health or genetic services, and the individual provided authorization;
- when the identity of specific employees was not disclosed;
- when the employer requested information to comply with Section 103 of the Family and Medical Leave Act; and
- when the employer purchased publically available documents that may have included family medical histories (books, magazines, etc).

Management of Genetic Information Specified

The bills would treat genetic information as part of the individual's confidential medical record, and require the employer to maintain separate forms or files for genetic information if they obtained it. Disclosure of information would be prohibited except when disclosure is:

- to the individual or employee at their request (including family members if family members are receiving services);
- to an occupational or other health researcher in compliance with 45 CFR Part 46;[53]
- in response to a court order when the employer has given the employee notice and sufficient time to challenge the order; and
- to government officials investigating compliance with Title II.

Limitations on disclosure would apply to the employer, employment agency, labor organization and labor-management committee. With regard to disclosure under a court order, the bills would limit disclosure to only the genetic information specifically authorized in the order, and would include an exception on disclosure made in connection to an employee's compliance with certification provisions of Section 103 of the Family and Medical Leave Act.

Study of Violations Required

S. 306 and H.R. 493 would not limit employees' rights or protections under the ADA or Rehabilitation Act of 1973 or any other federal or state statutes. The bills would establish a commission to review the science of genetics and make recommendations on whether the "disparate impact" is necessary to continue to protect individuals from situations where an employer (with no discriminatory intent) unwittingly violated the law, and as a result, disproportionate adverse effects are experienced by some individuals with certain genetic information. The bills would not apply to the Armed Forces Repository of Specimen Samples for the Identification of Remains.

Selected Legislative Issues

Debate about genetic nondiscrimination legislation has continued since such bills were first introduced in the 103rd Congress. In order to fully appreciate the debate, an understanding of how the HIPAA privacy rule currently governs insurers' and employers' use of health information is useful. The sections that follow present background about the privacy rule, and then present several of the issues that have been the topic of debate over time.

Privacy Rule Background

In general, the privacy rule covers all individually identifiable health information that is created or received by a health plan or health care provider, including genetic information and information about an individual's family medical history.[54] Plans and providers may use and disclose health information for their own treatment, payment, and other routine health care operations without patient authorization and with few restrictions. The rule, however, does not apply to other entities that collect and maintain health information such as financial institutions that offer life insurance. Employers that sponsor health plans on behalf of their employees present a challenge for the rule's implementation because of their interrelationship with the insurer or health maintenance organization (HMO) that typically administers the plan. In their role as plan sponsor, employers may seek health information to carry out various plan functions.

While the rule in general does not regulate employers, it does address the use and disclosure of health information (including genetic information) by *employers that sponsor group health plans*. The rule permits a group health plan, a health insurance issuer, or an HMO acting for a group health plan to disclose health information to a plan sponsor (employer), provided the plan documents are amended so that they limit the uses and disclosures of information by the sponsor to those consistent with the privacy rule. In addition, an employer must certify to a group health plan that it will not use the information for employment-related actions (e.g., hiring and promotion decisions). The employer must agree to establish adequate firewalls, so that only those employees that need health information to perform functions on behalf of the group health plan have access to such information.[55]

Title I: Is the Privacy Rule Sufficient to Protect Consumers?

S. 358 and H.R. 493 would extend privacy rule protections to insurance and employment functions to clarify the permitted uses of information as exchanged between plan sponsors (employers) and group health plans. Some have questioned whether these additional privacy and confidentiality provisions are necessary. Others have argued that while HIPAA addresses what to do with information that has already been obtained, the proposed bills would address more specifically the acquisition of information.

Titles I and II: Would Legislation Actually Increase Utilization?

Title II of S. 358 and H.R. 493 would require employers to keep genetic information in files separate from other employee medical information. This requirement would not apply to groups covered by Title I (health insurers), even those that are sponsored by employers as employee benefit packages, and would not affect the use of services within the group health plan. In previous Congresses, some expressed concern that the legislation, which was intended to increase utilization of health care services and participation in clinical studies, would actually reduce utilization because the overly burdensome separate file requirement would raise the cost of providing genetic services and would affect insurers' willingness to pay for them. Others argued that the separate file requirement was not particularly burdensome (the privacy rule already requires employers limit access to employees' protected health information). They further argued that the separate file requirement was restricted to employers and would not affect insurers or their customers.

Title I: Would the Minimum Penalty Encourage Frivolous Lawsuits?

The bills provide that, when Title I is violated and willful neglect is found, there is a minimum penalty of $2,500. For more severe or prolonged violations, the minimum penalty is $15,000. Some have argued that the establishment of a minimum penalty would increase the incentive for individuals to sue health plans for violations of privacy or denial of coverage based on genetic information, and could act as a disincentive for settling disagreements. Others have argued that the penalty clauses are equivalent to those contained in other civil rights legislation, and that appropriate penalties are necessary to deter discriminatory practices.

Title II: Do the Bills Specify How Information May Flow between a Group Health Plan and an Employer?

S. 358 and H.R. 493 generally prohibit employers from requesting or requiring genetic information about their employees. This is more restrictive than what HIPAA currently permits. HIPAA allows group health plans to disclose health information — including genetic information — to plan sponsors (employers) if certain conditions are met. The conditions are generally designed to allow sponsors to use the information to perform functions on behalf of the group health plan (i.e., administer the plan and develop of new insurance contracts), but not for employment-related actions (i.e., hiring and promotion decisions). Opponents of the legislation argue that such restrictions will create confusion regarding which types of health information insurers can release to employers, particularly if genetic information, which would have to be separated from other health information and be withheld from employers, is not clearly defined. Supporters of the legislation indicate that the bills would not change the foundation of protections established by HIPAA and the privacy rule. Instead, the net affect would be to build upon that foundation, to clarify the role of genetic information in the context of other health information, and to establish specific protections for genetic information for entities that are not described by HIPAA (e.g, plan sponsors).

Title II: Would the Bills Create an Incentive for Suing Employers?

The bills would permit individuals to sue without first filing a complaint with the EEOC. Some have argued that this, coupled with the absence of a cap on compensatory and punitive damages, would encourage frivolous litigation.[56] Others argue that, as with Title I, penalties are consistent with remedies under existing civil rights legislation (e.g., ADA), and argue that they are necessary to assure compliance with the provisions.

Title II: Do the Bills Strike the Right Balance between Public and Individual Risk?

S. 358 and H.R. 493 would not permit an employer to make an employment decision based on predictive genetic information, even when there may be some resulting risk to public health. OSHA currently has guidelines for monitoring for genetic changes associated with exposure in the workplace and susceptibility to exposure (29 C.F.R. Part 1910). Some argue that the bills should permit employers to make decisions based on predictive genetic information in situations where the public might be harmed (such as an employee carrying a gene predisposing him or her to epilepsy when the employee is a bus driver). Others stated that it was unfair to deny healthy people opportunities when only a possibility of becoming ill existed. Even if it could be known that a person would definitely become ill (as in the case with those that have a gene for Huntington's Disease), the precise time that the illness would prevent the employee from doing his or her job could not be known. Furthermore, they argue that allowing the use of predictive genetic information in these circumstances would create bias against those people who happened to be predisposed to a disease for which a test existed. If two people were genetically destined to become incapacitated at the same time, but by different diseases, and if there happened to be a predictive test developed for only one of the diseases, the person with a predisposition for that disease may be subject to adverse consequences from the availability of the information, while the other person would not.

Title II: Should the Bills Have a Sunset Clause?

S. 358 and H.R. 493 do not have a sunset clause. Some opponents argue that any genetic nondiscrimination legislation should have an expiration date to enable public policy to keep pace with scientific advances and allow Congress to decide how effectively the law has worked. This type of sunset clause is unusual in civil rights legislation; there is only one example of civil rights legislation that has an expiratory term.[57] Supporters of nondiscrimination legislation point out that Congress always reserves the right to evaluate the effectiveness of laws and make modifications as deemed necessary. Further, they do not believe that discrimination issues will go away in the near term. For example, a sunset provision may not protect a person who agreed to be tested when the laws were in effect, but whose genetic information would then be in his or her record after the laws expired.

Title II: Should the Bills Require Separate Medical Files?

S. 358 and H.R. 493 require employers to keep employees' genetic information in separate medical files. The House Committee on Education and Labor adopted an amendment to H.R. 493 on February 14, 2007, specifying that genetic information protected by the act could be maintained with and treated as a confidential medical record under ADA §102(d)(3)(B). S. 358 contains no parallel provision.

No federal or state law has a separate file requirement for group health plans acting to provide medical services, even though some studies show some physicians and genetics professionals are already keeping separate files in the absence of protecting legislation.[58] In fact, Executive Order 13145 already requires federal agencies, acting as employers, to maintain genetic information as part of their "confidential medical records which must be kept apart from personnel files." Some have argued that requiring maintenance of genetic information in separate files increases potential for medical error. Others point out that, because the language states that the requirement applies only to employers, the risk of medical error would only increase if Title II could be construed to include group health plans administering employer-sponsored benefits, which is contrary to precedent.

Title II: Should the Bills Create a Safe Harbor?

S. 358 and H.R. 493 would not preempt state laws. The legislation would set a floor of basic federal nondiscrimination regulations that would apply in all states, but would permit states to keep or enact their own more comprehensive genetic nondisrcrimination legislation. The bills would not provide a *safe harbor*, which would protect federally-compliant employers from prosecution under state genetic nondiscrimination laws. Because states vary widely in their approaches to genetic nondiscrimination, opponents of federal legislation proposed that any federal law should include a *safe harbor* provision. Supporters of the legislation argue that a federal floor is appropriate, and that states should continue to be able to enact and test the effects of additional genetic nondiscrimination provisions within their borders.

TITLE I AND TITLE II: HOW DO S. 358 AND H.R. 493 PROTECT GENETIC INFORMATION?

An overarching question regarding S. 358 and H.R. 493 is how the bills would protect genetic information. The answer depends both on types of protections (specifying what can be done with genetic information), and on the definition of genetic information itself (specifying what is protected and what is not). As discussed in previous sections, the types of protections would primarily be restrictions on the manner in which genetic information could be used in determining eligibility for health insurance, establishing premiums for health insurance, and in making decisions regarding employment. The definition of genetic information is discussed in detail below.

The bills define genetic information as — and therefore protect — knowledge derived from a genetic test performed on individuals or their family members that relates to the occurrence of a disease or disorder. The protections would apply to predictive genetic tests that provide information regarding a future possible health status of a currently non-affected person. The bills' precise definition of genetic information, and thus protections that they would provide, hinge on factors discussed below, including the definition of family medical history, differences between Title I and Title II, and predictive versus manifested disease information combined with the type of genetic test performed.

Family Medical History

S. 358 and H.R. 493 specify that genetic information includes the fact that an individual or his/her family member has taken a genetic test. The bills define family members to include distant relatives and adopted children (which have no blood relationship and therefore would not be affected by genetic information in the family). Historically, genetic nondiscrimination act bills have stressed the importance of family history. The Senate report to accompany S. 1053 (108th) stated that "the committee realizes that family medical history could be used as a surrogate for a genetic trait by a health plan or health insurance issuer ... it is important to include family medical history in the definition of genetic information."[59] The report further clarified the concept of family medical history as being consistent with the American Medical Association definition, and expected that the definition would evolve over time. Some debate has ensued over the question of who should be considered to be in one's family.

The risk of sharing genetic traits or conditions is greatest in first and second-degree blood relatives.[60] The risk of sharing genes decreases as the blood relationship becomes more distant. For example, first degree relatives share one-half of their genetic material, second degree relatives share one-fourth, and third degree relatives (first cousins), share one-eighth. Fourth cousins, which are ninth degree relatives, share only 1/512 of their genetic material. At this level of relationship, only very rare conditions appear more frequently in family members, and the risk of sharing many common diseases is virtually the same as in the general population.

Proponents of the legislation argue that the inclusion of individuals that have no blood relation (i.e., adoptive children) is necessary to insure that the family remains insurable as a unit; that adoptive children (or adoptive parents) are not penalized because one or the other has a genetic trait that they themselves could not have.

Opponents argued that inclusion of distant or non-blood related individuals further extends the potential for litigation against insurers or employers.[61]

The House Education and Labor Committee Chairman's version of H.R. 493 as reported by the committee defined a *family member* as someone related by blood within four generations. S. 358 contains no parallel provisions. During the February 14, 2007, House Education and Labor Committee markup, a proposed amendment to expand the definition of family member to include fetuses was defeated. However, the Chairman's amended version of the bill contains provisions in Title I and Title II specifying that the definition of *genetic information* (rather than *family member*) would include that of a fetus. S. 358 contains no similar provisions.

While prenatal testing may be either diagnostic or predictive in nature, coverage for a child does not usually begin until the moment of birth.[62] In general, medical insurance covers the named insured and dependents of the named insured. Any genetic information collected about a fetus while a woman is pregnant would likely arise in the context of providing prenatal care to the insured woman. Because the fetus would not appear to be a separate insured individual, it seems likely that any genetic information collected about the fetus would probably be attributed to the woman as the named insured, and protected from discrimination to the extent that her own medical information was protected.

Differences between Title I and Title II

The bills' two titles define genetic information differently and, therefore, apply different restrictions to employers and insurers. (See table 1). Title I (health insurance provisions) specifically excludes from its definition of genetic information — and therefore does not protect — medical information that is not genetic information, including the analysis of *proteins or metabolites directly related to manifested disease, disorder, or pathological condition.*

This exemption is not present in Title II (employment provisions), making the definition of genetic information — and the scope of what is protected — broader for employers than insurers. In addition, the bills would permit health insurers to use or disclose the individual's current health status (as determined without a genetic test), consistent with existing law. This permission is not present in Title II, as employers are already prohibited from using a person's current health status in specific ways by existing law.

Table 1. The Definition of Genetic Test and Genetic Information in Title I and Title II of S. 358 and H.R. 493

	Title I Health Insurance	Title II Employment
Genetic test	The term "genetic test" means the analysis of human DNA, RNA, chromosomes, proteins or metabolites that detects genotypes, mutations, or chromosomal changes.	Same as Title I.
Limitations or exemptions	"Genetic test" does not mean: (i) an analysis of proteins or metabolites that does not detect genotypes, mutations, or chromosomal changes; or (ii) an analysis of proteins or metabolites that is directly related to a manifested disease, disorder, or pathological condition that could reasonably be detected by a health care professional with appropriate training and expertise in the field of medicine involved.	"Genetic test" does not mean an analysis of proteins or metabolites that does not detect genotypes, mutations, or chromosomal changes.
Genetic information	"Genetic information" means: (i) information about an individual's genetic tests; (ii) information about genetic tests of family members of the individual; (ii) information about the occurrence of a disease or disorder in family members.	Same as Title I.
Limitations or exemptions	"Genetic information" does not include information about the age or sex of an individual.	Same as Title I.

Title I, Predictive vs. Manifested Disease Information and Type of Test

Title I of the bills focuses on protecting *predictive information* (i.e., information about a future or potential health state in a currently symptom-free individual). It does so by exempting from the definition of genetic information analyses of *proteins or metabolites* that are directly related to *manifested diseases*. Insurers could thus use this type of genetic information in accordance with current law governing insurance and employment practices. The definition of genetic test in the bills is more limited than the medical or scientific definition of genetic test, which covers both predictive and diagnostic reasons for testing.[63] Instances in which the distinction is blurred between predictive information and that related to a manifested disease may cause some confusion if the bills are enacted.

Based upon the definition of genetic test in Title II, analyses of a person's DNA or RNA would be protected regardless of whether any related disease had manifested. By contrast, as mentioned above, the definition of genetic test in Title I does not include analyses that are both conducted on *proteins or metabolites*, and are directly related to *manifested diseases*. Thus, information derived from studying a protein or metabolite would only be protected before symptoms appeared. These provisions create potentially unclear results when a single genetic test, which could be performed on DNA or proteins, yields results that are both related to a manifested disease or condition, and are predictive in nature. The potential dilemma is illustrated by the following example.

If a person had cancer, a test of the tumor DNA or proteins may simultaneously provide information about the tumor itself (a manifested disease), and its likelihood of recurrence (a predictive probability). If surgery were performed to remove the tumor and the patient went in to remission, the information obtained from the patients' tumor could be considered both diagnostic for the previously manifested tumor and predictive regarding a potential recurrence. If the test had been performed on tumor DNA, the information would be protected no matter whether it was considered to be diagnostic or predictive. However, if it had been performed on tumor proteins, if it were considered diagnostic it would not be protected. If it were considered predictive, it would be. (See table 2).

This same lack of clarity may create issues in the case in which a person undergoes a pharmacogenetic test, which is a genetic test to determine whether a person is susceptible to adverse reactions to or beneficial results from a certain drug or other treatment. Information from pharmacogenomic tests reveals normal variability in how different people's bodies process different medications —personalized medicine. It is unclear whether this type of test would be protected under current legislation. Pharmacogenetic tests for individual susceptibilities to certain drugs can be performed at any point in an individual's life (i.e., when an individual does not have a manifested disease). Thus, the scope of protections afforded to pharmacogenomic test results might depend on whether the person already had a disease for which the treatment was indicated. Under the current definition it is possible that, in the presence of manifested disease, information that a person would *not* likely respond to a drug could potentially be used in a negative manner by health insurers. This may be of particular concern if only one treatment exists.

Table 2. Examples of Genetic Testing Scenarios and Protected Information Under S. 358 and H.R. 493

Scenario	S. 358 and H.R. 493
Test of tumor proteins; information is diagnostic, the tumor has not been removed.	Not Protected because "analysis is of protein ... is directly related to a manifested disease."
Test of tumor DNA; information is diagnostic, the tumor has not been removed.	Protected, meets basic criteria for genetic test (only protein or metabolite tests meet exclusion for manifested disease).
Test of tumor proteins; tumor has been removed; information indicates the likelihood of tumor recurrence.	Not Protected if the removed tumor is a "manifested disease;" Protected if tumor removal means that the disease is no longer manifested.
Test of tumor DNA; tumor has been removed; information indicates the likelihood of tumor recurrence.	Protected, meets basic criteria for genetic test, so "manifested" is not an issue; limitation only applies to tests of protein.
Test of tumor protein; information requested for diagnostic purposes indicates resistence to therapy.	Not Protected if information about possible drug response is considered "directly related to manifested disease;" Protected if not directly related.
Test of tumor on patient's DNA; information requested for diagnostic purposes indicates resistence to therapy.	Protected, meets basic criteria for genetic test, so "directly related" is not an issue; (only protein or metabolite tests meet exclusion for manifested disease).

REFERENCES

[1] For a more detailed discussion of legal issues relating to the use of genetic information, see CRS Report RL30006, *Genetic Information: Legal Issues Relating to Discrimination and Privacy*, by Nancy Lee Jones and Amanda K. Sarata.

[2] The danger exists because certain genetic traits and predispositions can have higher frequencies among individuals of certain ethnic backgrounds. See Title VII of the Civil Rights Act, as amended by Civil Rights Act of 1991, P.L 102-166, Section 105(a), codified at 42 U.S.C. § 2000e-3(a); and *Norman-Bloodsaw v. Lawrence Berkeley Laboratory*, 135 F.3d 1260 (9th Cir. 1998).

[3] State information on privacy at [http://www.ncsl.org/programs/health/genetics/prt.htm] and employment at [http://www.ncsl.org/programs/health/genetics/ndiscrim.htm]. State information on insurance is at [http://www.genome.gov/PolicyEthics/ LegDatabase/ pubMap Search.cfm], and [http://www.ncsl.org/programs/health/genetics/ndishlth.htm]; accessed Mar. 5, 2007.

[4] M.A. Pagnattaro, "Genetic Discrimination and the Workplace: Employee's Right to Privacy vs Employer's Need to Know," *American Business Law Journal*, vol. 29 (2001), pp. 139-185.

[5] See the next section of this report for more discussion of the scope and types of information that could be used.

[6] U.S. Congress, Senate Committee on Health, Education, Labor, and Pensions, *Genetic Information Nondiscrimination Act of 2003*, report to accompany S. 1053, 108th Cong., 1st sess., S.Rept. 108-122, Genetic Information Nondiscrimination Act 2003

(Washington, GPO, 2003), pp.12-15. CRS Report RL30006, *Genetic Information: Legal Issues Related to Discrimination and Privacy*, by Nancy Lee Jones and Alison M. Smith.

[7] Sheryl Gay Stolberg. "President Calls for Genetic Privacy Bill," at [http://www.nytimes. com/2007/01/18/washington/18privacy.html?_r=1 and ref=health and oref=slogin#]; accessed January 18, 2007.

[8] The GINE Coalition is a business coalition of trade associations, professional organizations, individual companies and their representatives. In addition to the U.S. Chamber of Commerce, the coalition includes the Society for Human Resource Management (SHRM), the National Association of Manufacturers (NAM), the National Federation of Independent Business (NFIB) and the College and University Professional Association for Human Resources (CUPA-HR), among others. The exclusive focus of the GINE Coalition is the issue of genetic nondiscrimination in employment.

[9] Statement of Ronald Weich, on behalf of the American Civil Liberties Union, for inclusion in the record of the hearing of the Senate Committee on Health, Education, Labor and Pensions, July 25, 2001.

[10] Statement of the American Association of Health Plans Board of Directors, "Health Plan Principles Guide Policies Toward Genetic Testing and Treatments," Oct. 15, 2003, press release. The principles include the protection of all identifiable health information (including genetic information) from illegal use, prohibition from discrimination in insurance and employment based on health status, and use of genetic information to improve the quality of patient care [http://www.ahip.org/content/ pressrelease.aspx?docid=168], accessed Mar. 5, 2007.

[11] National Association of Health Underwriters, *Position on Genetic Testing*, at [http://www.nahu.org/legislative/Genetic_position.pdf]; accessed Mar. 3, 2007.

[12] David Hess, "Genetic Discrimination Bill Stalls in House," *Congress Daily*, Apr. 20, 2004.

[13] R.J. Ellis, et al., "Applying Diagnosis-Based Predictive Models to Group Underwriting," *Society of Actuaries Health Section News*, no. 46 (Aug. 2003), pp. 1, 4-7.

[14] J.A. Lowden, "Underwriting Lethal Genetic Diseases," *Journal of Insurance Medicine*, vol. 30, no. 1 (1998), pp. 5-11.

[15] Statement of Tom Miller, Director of Health Policy Studies, The Cato Institute, on Genetic Privacy before the Judiciary Subcommittee on the Constitution, U.S. House of Representatives, Sept. 12, 2002.

[16] J.V. Jacobi, "Genes and Disability: Defining Health and the Goals of Medicine: Genetic Discrimination in a Time of False Hopes," 30 Florida State University Law Review 363, Winter, 2003.

[17] Remarks of Paul Miller, Commissioner of the EEOC, "Analyzing Genetic Discrimination in the Workplace," at the EINSHAC International Working Conversation on Enviro/Genetics Disputes and Issues, July 2001.

[18] For a more detailed discussion of legal issues relating to the use of genetic information, see CRS Report RL30006, *Genetic Information: Legal Issues Relating to Discrimination and Privacy*, by Nancy L. Jones and Alison M. Smith.

[19] 29 C.F.R. Part 1910.

[20] P.G. Epps, "Policy Before Practice: Genetic Discrimination Reviewed," *American Journal of Pharmacogenomics*, vol. 3, no. 6, 2003, pp. 405-418.

[21] L. Plantinga et al., "Disclosure, Confidentiality, and Families: Experiences and Attitudes of Those with Genetic Versus Nongenetic Medical Conditions," *American Journal of Medicine, General Part C*, vol. 119C (2003), pp. 51-59.

[22] The information in this paragraph is from Shawna Williams, "The impact of genetic discrimination," *Genetics and Public Policy Center Issue Brief*, Oct. 24, 2006, at [http://www.dnapolicy.org/policy.issue.php?action=detail and issuebrief_id=34]; visited Jan. 6, 2007.

[23] Karen Rothenberg and Sharon Terry, "Before It's Too Late: Addressing Fear of Genetic Information," *Science*, vol. 297, no. 5579 (July 12, 2002), pp. 196-197.

[24] E. Virginia Lapham, Chahira Kozma, and Joan O. Weiss, "Genetic Discrimination: Perspectives of Consumers," *Science*, vol. 274, no. 5287 (Oct. 25, 1996), pp. 621-624.

[25] Testimony of the HIAA on Genetic Testing, in U.S. Congress, Senate Committee on Labor and Human Resources, 105th Cong., 2nd sess. (May 21, 1998).

[26] L.N. Geller, J.S. Alper, P.R. Billings, C.I. Barash, J. Beckwith, and M. Natowicz, "Individual, Family, and Societal Dimensions of Genetic Discrimination: A Case Study Analysis," *Science and Engineering Ethics*, vol. 2, no. 1, (1996), pp.71-88. See, also, the American Council of Life Insurance, "Statement Regarding the Council for Responsible Genetics 'Study' on Genetic Discrimination" (Apr. 11, 1996).

[27] Transcripts of the testimony can be found at [http://www4.od.nih.gov/oba/SACGHS/meetings/October2004/SACGHSOct2004postmeeting.htm]; accessed Mar. 5, 2007.

[28] Alpha-1 antitrypsin deficiency is a rare hereditary condition that results in lower production of a protein called alpha-1 antitrypsin. Alpha-1 antitrypsin circulates in the blood and protects the tissues of the body from being damaged by chemicals contained in white blood cells. Low levels of alpha-1 antitrypsin can result in lung and/or liver damage. The disease results when two copies of an abnormal gene are inherited — one from the mother and one from the father. When an individual inherits only one copy of an abnormal gene, they are known as "carriers."

[29] See Neil Osterweil, "Electronic Records, Private Lives: Who Gets a Peek at Online Medical Information?" Available at [http://my.webmd.com/content/article/ 74/ 89227.htm]; accessed Mar. 5, 2007.

[30] CRS Report RL30006, *Genetic Information: Legal Issues Relating to Discrimination and Privacy,* by Nancy Lee Jones and Alison M. Smith.

[31] M. A. Rothstein, "Genetics and the Work Force of the Next Hundred Years," *Columbia Business Law Review*, vol. 3 (2000), pp. 371-402, cited in P. G. Epps, "Policy Before Practice: Genetic Discrimination Reviewed," *American Journal of Pharmacogenomics*, vol. 3, no. 6, (2003), pp. 405-418.

[32] American Management Association, "Workplace Testing And Monitoring" (New York: American Management Association, 1998).

[33] American Management Association, "Workplace Testing: Medical Testing" (New York: American Management Association, 1999).

[34] American Management Association, "2001 AMA Survey: Medical Testing" (New York: American Management Association, 2001).

[35] Virginia E. Lapham, Chahira Kozma, and Joan O. Weiss, "Genetic Discrimination: Perspectives of Consumers," *Science*, vol. 274, no. 5287 (Oct. 25, 1996), pp. 621-624.

[36] Nancy E. Kass, et al., "Access to health insurance: Experiences and attitudes of those with genetic versus non-genetic medical conditions," *American Journal of Medical Genetics,* published in advance online Feb. 8, 2007, at [http://www3.interscience.wiley.com/cgi-bin/abstract/114114203/ABSTRACT]; visited Mar. 5, 2007.

[37] *EEOC v. Burlington N. Santa Fe Ry. Co.*, No.02-C-0456 (E.D. Wis. 2002).

[38] "Genetic Privacy and Discrimination" *Genetics and Public Policy Center Issue Brief*, at [http://www.dnapolicy.org/policy.privacy.php]; accessed Jan 8, 2007.

[39] Highlights and transcripts of testimony can be found on the SACGT website at [http://www4.od.nih.gov/oba/sacgt/sacgtmtg.htm]; accessed March 3, 2007.

[40] From a letter from SACGT to Secretary Tommy Thompson, May 3, 2001, at [http://www4.od.nih.gov/oba/sacgt/ltr_to_secDHHS5-3-01.pdf]; accessed Mar. 3, 2007.

[41] Testimony of SACGHS can be found at [http://www4.od.nih.gov/oba/SACGHS/meetings/October2004/SACGHSOct2004postmeeting.htm]; accessed Mar. 3, 2007.

[42] A genetic counselor is a health care professional who works very closely with a patient to explain genetic testing options, interpret test results and explain the implications of genetic information to that patient and their family.

[43] E.T. Matloff et al., "What Would You Do? Specialists' Perspectives on Cancer Genetic Testing, Prophylactic Surgery, and Insurance Discrimination," *Journal of Clinical Oncology*, vol. 18, no. 1 (June 2000), pp. 2484-2492.

[44] S. E. Applebaum-Shapiro, et al., "Motivations and Concerns of Patients with Access to Genetic Testing for Hereditary Pancreatitis," *American Journal Gastroenterology*, vol. 96, no. 5 (2001), pp. 1610-1617.

[45] H.T. Lynch et al., "Hereditary Breast-ovarian Cancer at the Bedside: Role of the Medical Oncologist," *Journal of Clinical Oncology*, vol. 21, no. 4 (Feb. 15, 2003), pp. 740-753.

[46] E.A. Peterson et al., "Health Insurance and Discrimination Concerns and BRCA1/2 Testing in a Clinic Population," *Cancer Epid., Biomarkers and Prev.*, vol. 11 (Jan. 2002), pp. 79-82.

[47] S.C. Lee, B.A. Bernhardt, and K.J. Helzlsouer, "Utilization of BRCA1/2 Genetic Testing in the Clinical Setting," *Cancer*, vol. 94, no. 6 (Mar. 15, 2002), pp. 1876-1885.

[48] M.A. Hall and S.S. Rich, "Genetic Privacy Laws and Patients' Fear of Discrimination by Health Insurers: the View from Genetic Counselors," *Journal of Law, Medicine and Ethics*, vol. 28, no. 3 (fall 2000), pp. 245-257. (Hereafter cited as M.A. Hall and S.S. Rich, "Genetic Privacy Laws.")

[49] M.A. Hall and S.S. Rich, "Genetic Privacy Laws." See, also, references and endnotes 14-16 therein.

[50] Ibid.

[51] Ibid.

[52] For further information about HIPAA, see CRS Report RL31634, *The Health Insurance Portability and Accountability Act (HIPAA) of 1996: Overview and Guidance on Frequently Asked Questions*, by Hinda Chaikind, Bob Lyke, C. Stephen Redhead, and Jean Hearne, at [http://www.congress.gov/erp/rl/pdf/RL31634.pdf]; accessed Mar. 3, 2007.

[53] 45 C.F.R. Part 46 contains the Department of Health and Human Service's regulations governing the protection of human subjects in research. Subpart A of these regulations

is known as the "Common Rule" because 17 other federal agencies have adopted parallel requirements.

[54] For further information about the HIPAA Rule, see CRS Report RS20500, *Medical Records Privacy: Questions and Answers on the HIPAA Privacy Rule*, by C. Stephen Redhead.

[55] 45 C.F.R. 164.504(f). The rule permits the following types of disclosure of health information to a plan sponsor without amending the plan documents: (1) disclosure of summary information (identifiers removed), if requested, for the purpose of obtaining premium bids or modifying, amending or terminating the group plan; and (2) disclosure of information on whether an individual is enrolled in or has disenrolled from a plan.

[56] Letter from J.C. McGuiness, President, to LPA Primary Reps, LPA Washington Reps and the LPA Labor Law Group, "A Solution in Search of a Problem: Congress Considering Legislation to Ban Nonexistent Genetic Discrimination," June 4, 2003.

[57] There are provisions in the 1965 Voting Rights Act which must be periodically extended. For example, Section 203 requires bilingual voting services in certain states and political subdivisions with significant numbers of non-English speaking citizens. The voting rights act was last reauthorized in 2006, and extended for a period of 25 years. P.L. 109-246; see 42 U.S.C. 1973aa-1a.

[58] M.A. Hall and S.S. Rich, "Genetic privacy laws and patients' fear of discrimination by health insurers: the view from genetic counselors," *Journal of Law, Medicine and Ethics*, vol. 28, no. 3, fall 2000, pp. 245-257.

[59] S.Rept. 108-122 for S. 1053 (108th).

[60] A first degree relative is defined as a parent, brother, sister, or child of an individual. A second degree relative would include grandparents, aunts, uncles, nephews, or nieces (children of aunts and uncles) of an individual. First cousins (children of brothers and sisters) are third degree relatives of an individual. Second cousins are fifth degree relatives. Third cousins are seventh degree relatives. Even degrees, such as fourth and sixth, refer to different generations, i.e., "first cousins once removed."

[61] A related question is whether or not information derived from genetic tests performed on a fetus or parental material from in vitro fertilization procedures (e.g., polar bodies or pre-implantation embryos) would be protected, insofar as blood relatives are concerned. Since predictive testing for adult diseases is not currently recommended in prenatal situations, presumably the information gained from such testing would be diagnostic for the fetus or embryo. However, such diagnosis could provide genetic information about parents, siblings and other blood relatives, which presumably then could be used by health insurers or employers in making insurance or employment decisions for other individuals in the family.

[62] *See* Lee R. Russ, *Couch on Insurance, 3rd ed.*, § 144:28 (Andover, UK: Sweet and Maxwell Ltd., 2005).

[63] For reference, the medical definition of genetic test includes the analysis of human proteins and certain metabolites, which are predominantly used to detect heritable or acquired genotypes (reflective of the individual's DNA), mutations (actual changes in DNA from the "normal" sequence), or phenotypes (a trait which is visible). This definition covers both diagnostic and predictive information with respect to current or future health status.

In: Genetic Discrimination
Editor: Leana J. Albertson, pp. 31-40
ISBN: 978-1-60456-357-3

Chapter 2

GENETIC TESTING: SCIENTIFIC BACKGROUND FOR POLICYMAKERS*

Amanda K. Sarata

ABSTRACT

In the 109th Congress, several pieces of legislation were introduced that related to genetic and genomic technology and testing, including the Genetic Information Nondiscrimination Act of 2005 (S. 306/H.R. 1227), the Genomics and Personalized Medicine Act of 2006 (S. 3822) and the Prenatally Diagnosed Condition Awareness Act (S. 609). Although none of these bills passed, they signal the growing importance of the public policy issues surrounding the clinical and public health implications of new genetic technology. As genetic technologies proliferate and are increasingly used to guide clinical treatment, these public policy issues are likely to continue to garner considerable attention. Understanding the basic scientific concepts underlying genetics and genetic testing may help facilitate the development of more effective public policy in this area.

Most diseases have a genetic component. Some diseases such as Huntington's Disease are caused by a specific gene. Other diseases, such as heart disease and cancer, are caused by a complex combination of genetic and environmental factors. For this reason, the public health burden of genetic disease is substantial, as is its clinical significance. Experts note that society has recently entered a transition period in which specific genetic knowledge is becoming critical to the delivery of effective health care for everyone. Therefore, the value of and role for genetic testing in clinical medicine is likely to increase significantly in the future.

INTRODUCTION

Virtually all disease has a genetic component.[1] The term "genetic disease" has traditionally been used to refer to rare monogenic (caused by a single gene) inherited disease,

* Excerpted from CRS Report RL33832, dated January 26, 2007.

for example, cystic fibrosis. However, we now know that all complex diseases, including common chronic conditions such as cancer, heart disease and diabetes, are the product of some combination of genetic and environmental factors. For this reason, they could all be said to be "genetic diseases". Considering this broader definition of genetic disease, the public health burden of genetic disease can be seen to be substantial. In addition, an individual patient's genetic make-up, and the genetic make-up of his disease, will help guide clinical decision making. Experts note that "(w)e have recently entered a transition period in which specific genetic knowledge is becoming critical to the delivery of effective health care for everyone."[2] For this reason, the value of and role for genetic testing in clinical medicine is likely to increase significantly in the future. As the role of genetics in clinical medicine and public health continues to grow, so will the importance of public policy issues raised by genetic technologies.

Science is only beginning to unlock the complex nature of the interaction between genes and the environment in common disease, and their respective contributions to the disease process. The information gleaned from the Human Genome Project will help, and is currently helping, scientists and clinicians to identify common genetic variation that contributes to disease. In addition, research conducted utilizing large population databases that collect health, genetic, and environmental information about entire populations will likely provide more information about the genetic and environmental underpinnings of common diseases. Many countries have established such databases, including Iceland, the United Kingdom, and Estonia. The knowledge of the potential relevance of genetic information to the clinical management of nearly all patients coupled with the lack of complete information about the genetic and environmental factors underlying disease creates a challenging climate for public policymaking.

In many cases, the results of genetic testing may be used to guide clinical management of patients. For example, more frequent screening may be recommended for individuals at increased risk of certain diseases by virtue of their genetic make-up, such as colorectal and breast cancer. In some cases, prophylactic surgery may even be indicated. Decisions about courses of treatment and dosing may also be guided by genetic testing, as might reproductive decisions (both clinical and personal). However, many diseases do not have any treatment available (for example, Huntington's Disease). In these cases, the benefits of genetic testing lie largely in the information they provide an individual about his or her risk of future disease or current disease status. The value of genetic information in these cases is personal to individuals, who may choose to utilize this information to help guide medical and other life decisions for themselves and their families. The information can affect decisions about reproduction, the types or amount of health, life, or disability insurance to purchase, or career and education choices. As genetic research continues to advance rapidly, it will often be the case that genetic testing may be able to provide information about the probability of a health outcome without an accompanying treatment option. This situation again creates unique public policy challenges, for example, in terms of the financing of genetic testing services and education about the value of testing (see S. 609, 109th Congress, for example).

Concerns about privacy and the use and misuse of genetic information, as well as issues of genetic exceptionalism[3] and genetic determinism[4], may need to be balanced with the potential of genetics and genetic technology to change how care is delivered and to personalize medical care and treatment of disease.

This report will summarize basic scientific concepts in genetics and will provide an overview of genetic tests, their main characteristics, and the key policy issues they raise.

FUNDAMENTAL CONCEPTS IN GENETICS

The following section explains key concepts in genetics that are essential for understanding genetic testing and issues associated with testing that are of interest to Congress.

Cells Contain Chromosomes

Humans have 23 pairs of chromosomes in the nucleus of most cells in their bodies. These include 22 pairs of autosomal chromosomes (numbered 1 through 22) and one pair of sex chromosomes (X and Y). One copy of each autosomal chromosome is inherited from the mother and from the father, and each parent contributes one sex chromosome.

Many syndromes involving abnormal human development result from abnormal numbers of chromosomes (such as Down Syndrome). Other diseases, such as leukemia, can be caused by breaks in or rearrangements of chromosome pieces.

Chromosomes Contain DNA

Chromosomes are composed of deoxyribonucleic acid (DNA) and protein. DNA is comprised of complex chemical substances called bases. Strands made up of combinations of the four bases (adenine (A), guanine (G), cytosine (C) and thymine (T)) twist together to form a double helix (like a spiral staircase). Chromosomes contain almost 3 billion base pairs of DNA that code for about 20,000-25,000 genes (this is a current estimate, although it may change and has changed several times since the publication of the human genome sequence).[5]

DNA Codes for Protein

Proteins are fundamental components of all living cells. They include enzymes, structural elements, and hormones. Each protein is made up of a specific sequence of amino acids. This sequence of amino acids is determined by the specific order of bases in a section of DNA. A gene is the section of DNA which contains the sequence which corresponds to a specific protein. Changes to the DNA sequence, called mutations, can change the amino acid sequence. Thus, variations in DNA sequence can manifest as variations in the protein which may affect the function of the protein. This may result in, or contribute to the development of, a genetic disease.

Genotype Influences Phenotype

Though most of the genome is very similar between individuals, there can be significant variation in physical appearance or function between individuals. In other words, although we share most of the genetic material we have, we can see that there are significant differences in our physical appearance (height, weight, eye color, etc.). Humans inherit one copy (or allele) of most genes from each parent. The specific alleles that are present on a chromosome pair constitute a person's genotype. The actual observable physical trait is known as the phenotype. For example, having two brown-eye color alleles would be an example of a genotype and having brown eyes would be the phenotype.

Many complex factors affect how a genotype (DNA) translates to a phenotype (observable trait) in ways that are not yet clear for many traits or conditions. Study of a person's genotype may determine if a person has a mutation associated with a disease, but only observation of the phenotype can determine if that person actually has physical characteristics or symptoms of the disease. Generally, the risk of developing a disease caused by a single mutation can be more easily predicted than the risk of developing a complex disease caused by multiple mutations in multiple genes and environmental factors. Complex diseases, such as heart disease, cancer, immune disorders, or mental illness, for example, have both inherited and environmental components that are very difficult to separate. Thus, it can be difficult to determine whether an individual will develop symptoms, how severe the symptoms may be, or when they may appear.

Genetic Tests

What Is a Genetic Test?

Scientifically, a genetic test is defined as:

> "an analysis performed on human DNA, RNA, genes, and/or chromosomes to detect heritable or acquired genotypes, mutations, phenotypes, or karyotypes that cause or are likely to cause a specific disease or condition. A genetic test also is the analysis of human proteins and certain metabolites, which are predominantly used to detect heritable or acquired genotypes, mutations, or phenotypes."[6]

Once the sequence of a gene is known, looking for specific changes is relatively straightforward using the modern techniques of molecular biology. In fact, these methods have become so advanced that hundreds or thousands of genetic variations can be detected simultaneously using a technology called a microarray.

Policy Issues

The way genetic test is defined is extremely important to the development of genetics-related public policy. For example, the above scientific definition is very broad and inclusive, but this may not be the best way to achieve certain policy goals. It may sometimes be desirable to limit the definition only to predictive, and not diagnostic, genetic testing (see "What are the different Types of Genetic Tests?"). In other cases, it may be desirable to limit the definition to only analysis of specific material, such as DNA, RNA, and chromosomes, but not metabolites or proteins. Considerable variation in the definition of genetic test may be found in the many state genetic nondiscrimination laws. Policies extending protection against discrimination may aim to be as broad as possible, whereas policies addressing coverage of genetic tests may aim to be more limited.

How Many Genetic Tests Are Available?

As of January 5, 2007, genetic tests were available for 1,343 diseases. Of those tests, 1,046 were available for clinical diagnosis, while 297 were available for research only.[7] The majority of these tests are for single-gene rare diseases. Asked about the realistic promise of genetic technology, Francis Collins, the Director of the National Human Genome Research Institute predicted,

> "I think we can count on the availability within the next decade of a panel of genetic tests that are going to be offered to all of us to determine our risk of common illnesses, focused particularly on those diseases for which there is some intervention available for those found to be at high risk."[8]

What Are the Different Types of Genetic Tests?

Most clinical genetic tests are for rare disorders, but increasingly, tests are becoming available to determine susceptibility to common, complex diseases and to predict response to medication.

With respect to health-related tests (i.e., excluding tests used for forensic purposes, such as "DNA fingerprinting"), there are two general types of genetic testing: diagnostic and predictive. Genetic tests can be utilized to identify the presence or absence of a disease (diagnostic). Predictive genetic tests can be used to predict if an individual will definitely get a disease in the future (predictive-presymptomatic) or to predict the risk of an individual getting a disease in the future (predictive- predispositional). For example, testing for mutations in the BRCA1 and/or BRCA2 genes provides probabilistic information about how likely an individual is to develop breast cancer in his or her lifetime (predispositional). The genetic test for Huntington's Disease provides genetic information that is predictive in that it allows a physician to predict with certainty whether an individual will develop the disease, but does not allow the physician to determine when the onset of symptoms will actually occur (presymptomatic). In both of these examples, the individual does not have the clinical disease at the time of genetic testing, as they would with diagnostic genetic testing.

Within this broader framework of diagnostic and predictive genetic tests, several distinct types of genetic testing can be considered. Reproductive genetic testing can identify carriers of genetic disorders, establish prenatal diagnoses or prognoses, or identify genetic variation in embryos before they are used in in vitro fertilization. Reproductive testing, such as prenatal testing, may be either diagnostic or predictive in nature. Newborn screening is a type of genetic testing that identifies newborns with certain metabolic or inherited conditions (although not all newborn screening tests are genetic tests). Traditionally, most newborn screening has been diagnostic, but recently several states have added some predictive genetic testing to their panels of newborn screening (for example, Maryland includes testing for cystic fibrosis).[9] Finally, pharmacogenomic testing, or testing to determine a patient's likely response to a medication, may be considered either diagnostic or predictive, depending on the context in which it is being utilized.

Policy Issues

Generally, predictive genetic testing (both presymptomatic and predispositional), rather than diagnostic testing, raises more complex ethical, legal and social issues. For example, issues surrounding insurance coverage and reimbursement for this type of test, especially if no treatment is available, are far more complex than with diagnostic genetic testing. A private insurer may feel that paying for a test that predicts the onset of a disease with no treatment is not cost-effective. Even more complicated are cases where the test only shows an increased probability of getting a disease. In addition, Medicare's screening exclusion means that this type of test generally will not be covered for the elderly population.[10]

Another issue is the oversight of genetic tests. Strong oversight of genetic tests may be more important where the information is probabilistic rather than diagnostic and when a treatment is not available. Finally, issues of genetic discrimination may be different with predictive testing than they are with diagnostic testing. Genetic discrimination may be defined as differential treatment in either health insurance coverage or employment based upon an individual's genotype. Discriminatory action based on the possibility of something happening in the future, or even the certainty of it happening in the future, might raise more concern than would action taken based upon diagnostic information. With probabilistic genetic information, the health outcome of concern may never manifest, or if it is certain to, may not manifest for decades into the future.

The Genetic Test Result

Genetic tests can provide information about both inherited genetic variations, that is, the individual's genes that were inherited from their mother and father, as well as about acquired genetic variations, such as those that cause some tumors. Acquired mutations are not inherited, but rather are acquired in DNA due to replication errors or exposure to mutagenic chemicals and radiation (e.g., UV rays).

DNA-based testing of inherited genetic variants differs from other medical testing in important ways: it can have exceptionally long-range predictive powers over the lifespan of an individual; it can predict disease or increased risk for disease in the absence of clinical signs or symptoms; it can reveal the sharing of genetic variants within families at precise and calculable rates; and, at least theoretically, it has the potential to generate a unique identifier profile for individuals. Also, unlike most other medical tests, the stability of DNA means that most genetic tests can be performed on material from a body and continue to provide information after the individual has died.

Genetic changes to inherited genes can be acquired throughout a person's life. Tests that are performed for acquired genetic markers that occur with a disease have implications only for individuals with the disease, and not family members. Tests for acquired genetic changes are also usually diagnostic rather than predictive, since these tests are generally performed after symptoms present.

Pharmacogenomic testing may be used to determine acquired genetic variations in disease tissue (i.e., acquired variations in a tumor) or may be used to determine inherited variations in an individual's drug metabolizing enzymes. For example, with respect to determining acquired variation in disease tissue, a tumor may have acquired genetic changes that make it different from normal tissue that may also render that tumor susceptible or resistant to chemotherapy. With respect to inherited variation in drug metabolizing enzymes, an individual may be found to be a slow metabolizer of a certain type of drug (statins, for example) and this information can be used to guide both drug choice and dosing.

Policy Issues

In some cases, people feel differently about their genetic information than they do about other medical information, a sentiment embodied by the concept of genetic exceptionalism. This may be based on the stated differences between genetic testing and other medical testing, but also may be based on personal belief that genetic information is powerful and different than other medical information. For this reason, public policies around genetic discrimination in health insurance, employment and sometimes life insurance proliferated at the state level in the 1990s, and genetic nondiscrimination legislation has been considered by Congress for nearly a decade. Whether genetic information is somehow different from other medical information; whether it can be separated logically from other medical information; and whether it deserves special protection are all important public policy issues.

Pharmacogenomic testing is important because it will help provide the foundation for personalized medicine. Personalized medicine is healthcare based on individualized diagnosis and treatment for each patient determined by information at the genomic level. Many public policy issues are associated with personalized medicine. For example, there is some uncertainty currently as to how health insurers will assess and choose to cover pharmacogenomic testing as it becomes available. In addition, there are issues surrounding the regulation of pharmacogenomic testing. The Genomics and Personalized Medicine Act of 2006 (S. 3822, 109th Congress) considered many of these issues.

Characteristics of Genetic Tests

Genetic tests function in two environments: the laboratory and the clinic. Genetic tests are evaluated based primarily on three characteristics: analytical validity, clinical validity, and clinical utility.

Analytical Validity. Analytical validity is defined as the ability of a test to detect or measure the analyte it is intended to detect or measure.[11] This characteristic is critical for all clinical laboratory testing, not only genetic testing, as it provides information about the ability of the test to perform reliably at its most basic level. This characteristic is relevant to how well a test performs in a laboratory.

Clinical Validity. The clinical validity of a genetic test is its ability to accurately diagnose or predict the risk of a particular clinical outcome. A genetic test's clinical validity relies on an established connection between the DNA variant being tested for and a specific health outcome. Clinical validity is a measure of how well a test performs in a clinical rather than laboratory setting. Many measures are used to assess clinical validity, but the two of key importance are clinical sensitivity and positive predictive value. Genetic tests can be either diagnostic or predictive and, therefore, the measures used to assess the clinical validity of a genetic test must take this into consideration. For the purposes of a genetic test, positive predictive value can be defined as the probability that a person with a positive test result (i.e., the DNA variant tested for is present) either has or will develop the disease the test is designed to detect. Positive predictive value is the test measure most commonly used by physicians to gauge the usefulness of a test to clinical management of patients. Determining the positive predictive value of a predictive genetic test may be difficult because there are many different DNA variants and environmental modifiers that may affect the development of a disease. In other words, a DNA variant may have a known association with a specific health outcome, but it may not always be causal. Clinical sensitivity may be defined as the probability that people who have, or will develop a disease, are detected by the test.

Clinical Utility. Clinical utility takes into account the impact and usefulness of the test results to the individual and family and primarily considers the implications that the test results have for health outcomes (for example, is treatment or preventive care available for the disease). It also includes the utility of the test more broadly for society, and can encompass considerations of the psychological, social and economic consequences of testing.

Policy Issues

These three characteristics of genetic tests have important ties to public policy issues. For example, although the analytical validity of genetic tests is regulated by the Centers for Medicare and Medicaid Services (CMS) through the Clinical Laboratory Improvement Amendments (CLIA) of 1988 (P.L. 100-578), the clinical validity of the majority of genetic tests is not regulated at all. This has raised concerns about direct-to-consumer marketing of genetic tests where the connection between a DNA variant and a clinical outcome has not been clearly established. Marketing of such tests to consumers directly may mislead consumers into believing that the advice given them based on the results of such tests could improve their health status/outcomes when in fact there is no scientific basis underlying such an assertion. This issue was the subject of a July 2006 hearing by the Senate Special Committee on Aging. In addition, clinical utility and clinical validity both figure prominently into coverage decisions by payers, but a lack of data often hinders coverage decisions, leaving patients without coverage for these expensive tests.

Coverage by Health Insurers

Health insurers are playing an increasingly large role in determining which medical tests are available by deciding which tests they will pay for as part of patient benefit packages. Many aspects of genetic tests, including their clinical validity and utility, may complicate the coverage decision-making process for insurers. While insurers require that a test be approved by the Food and Drug Administration (when required), they also want evidence that it is "medically necessary;" that is, evidence demonstrating that a test will affect a patient's health outcome in a positive way. This additional requirement of evidence of improved health outcomes underscores the importance of patient participation in long-term research in genetic medicine. Particularly for genetic tests, data on health outcomes may take a very long time to collect.

Policy Issues

Decisions by insurers to cover new genetic tests have a significant impact on the utilization of such tests and their eventual integration into the health care system. The integration of personalized medicine into the health care system will be significantly affected by coverage decisions. Although insurers are beginning to cover pharmacogenomic tests and treatments, the high cost of such tests and treatments often means that insurers require very stringent evidence that they will improve health outcomes. In addition, the fact that Medicare does not routinely cover preventive services (unless authorized specifically by Congress) means that coverage for many genetic tests and services, which may be considered preventive, may not be granted under Medicare. As Medicare coverage decisions are often looked to by private insurers as a guide for their own coverage decisions, it is difficult to predict what effect this might have on the uptake and utilization of genetic tests more broadly.

Regulation of Genetic Tests by the Federal Government

Genetic tests are regulated by the FDA and CMS through CLIA. FDA regulates genetic tests that are manufactured by industry and sold for clinical diagnostic use. These test kits usually come prepackaged with all of the reagents and instructions that a laboratory needs to perform the test and are considered to be products by the FDA. FDA requires manufacturers of the kits to make sure that the test detects what they say it will, in the patient population in which they intend the test to be used. With respect to the characteristics of a genetic test, this process requires manufacturers to prove that their test is clinically valid. Depending on the perceived risk associated with the intended use promoted by the manufacturer, genetic tests must either prove that they are safe and effective, or that they are substantially equivalent to something that is already on the market that has the same intended use.

Most genetic tests are performed, not with test kits, but rather as laboratory testing services (or "homebrew" tests), meaning that clinical laboratories themselves perform the test in-house and make most or all of the reagents used in the tests. Homebrew tests are not currently regulated by the FDA in the way kits are and, therefore, the clinical validity of the vast majority of genetic tests is not regulated. The FDA does regulate certain components used in homebrew tests, known as Analyte Specific Reagents (ASRs), if the ASR is commercially available. If the ASR is made in-house by a laboratory performing a homebrew test, the test is not regulated at all by the FDA. This type of test is known as a "homebrew-homebrew" test.

Any clinical test that is performed with results returned to the patient must be performed in a CLIA-certified laboratory. CLIA is primarily administered by CMS in conjunction with the Centers for Disease Control and Prevention (CDC) and the FDA.[12] FDA determines the category of complexity of the test so that laboratories know which parts of CLIA they must follow. As previously noted, CLIA regulates the analytical validity of a clinical laboratory test only. It generally establishes requirements for laboratory processes, such as personnel training and quality control/quality assurance programs. CLIA requires laboratories to prove that their tests work properly, to maintain the appropriate documentation, and to show that tests are interpreted by laboratory professionals with the appropriate training. However, CLIA does not require that tests made by laboratories undergo any review by an outside agency to see if they work properly. Proponents of CLIA argue that regulation of the testing process gives the laboratories optimal flexibility to modify tests as new information becomes available. Critics argue that CLIA does not go far enough to assure the accuracy of genetic tests since it only addresses analytical validity and not clinical validity.

References

[1] Collins FS and McCusick VA. (2001) "Implications of the Human Genome Project for Medical Science." *Journal of the American Medical Association* 285: 540-544.

[2] Guttmacher AE and FS Collins. (2002) "Genomic medicine- A Primer." *New England Journal of Medicine* 347(19):1512-1520.

[3] *Genetic exceptionalism* is the concept that genetic information is inherently unique, should receive special consideration, and should be treated differently from other medical information.

[4] *Genetic determinism* is the concept that our genes are our destiny and that they solely determine our behavioral and physical characteristics. This concept has mostly fallen out of favor as the substantial role of the environment in determining characteristics has been recognized.

[5] National Research Council, Reaping the Benefits of Genomic and Proteomic Research: Intellectual Property Rights, Innovation, and Public Health (Washington, DC: National Academies Press (2006)); Page 19.

[6] Report of the Secretary's Advisory Committee on Genetic Testing (SACGT), "*Enhancing the Oversight of Genetic Tests: Recommendations of the SACGT,"* July 2000, at [http://www4.od.nih.gov/oba/sacgt/reports/oversight_report.pdf]. Accessed Jan. 5, 2007.

[7] Gene Tests. [http://www.genetests.org]. Accessed Jan. 5, 2007.

[8] E. Rabinowitz, "Genetics in Medicine: Hype or Real Promise?" *Health plan*, Jan./Feb. 2003.

[9] Newborn Screening Programs, Family Health Administration, Maryland Department of Health and Mental Hygiene. Accessed on Jan. 5, 2007, at [http://www.fha.state.md.us/genetics/html/nbs_ndx.html]

[10] Secretary's Advisory Committee on Genetics, Health, and Society. "Coverage and Reimbursement of Genetic Tests and Services." February 2006. Accessed on January 5, 2007 at [http://www4.od.nih.gov/oba/sacghs/reports/CR_report.pdf]. CMS has interpreted the Medicare statute to exclude coverage of preventive care unless specifically authorized by Congress.

[11] An analyte is defined as a substance or chemical constituent undergoing analysis.

[12] See [http://www.cms.hhs.gov/CLIA/08_Waived_PPMP_Laboratory_Project.asp]. Accessed on Oct. 16, 2006.

In: Genetic Discrimination
Editor: Leana J. Albertson, pp. 41-60
ISBN: 978-1-60456-357-3

Chapter 3

GENETIC INFORMATION: LEGAL ISSUES RELATING TO DISCRIMINATION AND PRIVACY*

Nancy Lee Jones and Alison M. Smith

ABSTRACT

In April 2003, the finished sequence of the human genome was deposited into public databases. This milestone, which has been compared to the discoveries of Galileo, and other advances in genetics have created novel legal issues relating to genetic information. The Human Genome Project, which produced detailed maps of the 23 pairs of human chromosomes and sequenced 99% of the three billion nucleotide bases that make up the human genome, has been instrumental in the identification of genes implicated in various diseases including glaucoma, colon cancer, and cystic fibrosis. With the identification of these genes comes the hope of genetic therapies to cure disease but this scientific accomplishment is not without potential problems. For instance the presence of a cancer causing gene may indicate a predisposition but does not guarantee that the person will contract the disease: How should an employer or insurer respond? The ethical, social and legal implications of these technological advances have been the subject of significant scrutiny and concern.

The legal implications of such information have been addressed in various ways largely by states, but also by Congress. The Health Insurance Portability and Accountability Act of 1996, P.L. 104-191, is the first federal law to specifically address discrimination and insurance issues relating to genetic discrimination. Congress has considered several bills concerning genetics during the past several Congresses. In the 109th Congress, S. 306, the Genetic Information Nondiscrimination Act of 2005, was passed on February 17, 2005 by a vote of 98-0. A companion bill, H.R. 1227, was introduced on March 10, 2005. In the 108th Congress, the Senate passed the Genetic Information Nondiscrimination Act of 2003, S. 1053. H.R. 1910 was introduced in the House and hearings were held but the bill was not passed in the 108th Congress. This report discusses current federal law, state statutes, and legislation. It will be updated as needed.

---

* Excerpted from CRS Report RL30006, dated March 11, 2005.

BACKGROUND

In April 2003, the finished sequence of the human genome was deposited into public databases. More specifically, the scientists involved in the Human Genome Project (HGP)[1] reported that the finished sequence consists of overlapping fragments covering 99% of the gene-containing portion of the human genome, with an accuracy of 99.999%.[2] These rapid advances provide powerful tools for information about the causes, and potentially the cures, for diseases such as diabetes, heart disease, Parkinson's disease, bipolar illness, and asthma.

In congressional testimony Dr. Francis Collins, the Director of the National Human Genome Research Institute, described the dramatic progress of the Human Genome Project and stated that "these revelations hold within them the promise of a true transformation of medical practice. Quite possibly before the end of the first decade of this new millennium, each of us may be able to learn our individual susceptibilities to common disorders, in some cases allowing the design of a program of effective individualized preventive medicine focused on lifestyle changes, diet and medical surveillance to keep us healthy....These same discoveries about genetics likely will lead us to predict who will respond most effectively to a particular drug therapy, and who may suffer a side effect and out to avoid that particular drug."[3]

Collectively, genetic diseases and common diseases with a genetic component pose a significant public health burden. With completion of the human genome sequence, scientists will now focus on understanding the clinical implications of the sequence information. As predicted by Dr. Collins, clinical genetic tests are becoming available at a rapid rate and are beginning to be included in health insurance benefits packages.[4]

The first apparently successful genetic therapy has been recently reported[5] and in the not too distant future, the benefits of genetic therapy have been seen by some as little short of miraculous with potential cures of major diseases such as heart disease, and cancer, and Alzheimer's. However, there have been numerous ineffective efforts at gene therapy and at Senate hearings, held following the death of a patient involved in gene therapy, Senator Frist stated that gene therapy holds "great promise, but because gene therapy is an experimental, high risk procedure, there is a need for vigilant oversight to ensure patient safety."[6]

These scientific advances in genetics are not without other potential problems. The ethical, social and legal implications of genetic research have been the subject of significant scrutiny and a portion of the funds for the Human Genome Project are set aside for use in analyzing these issues.[7] As scientific knowledge about genetics becomes increasingly widespread, numerous researchers and commentators, including Dr. Francis Collins, have expressed concerns about how this information is to be used.[8] In recent congressional testimony, Dr. Collins stated: "while genetic information and genetic technology hold great promise for improving human heath, they can also be used in ways that are fundamentally unjust. Genetic information can be used as the basis for insidious discrimination....The misuse of genetic information has the potential to be a very serious problem, both in terms of people's access to employment and health insurance and the continued ability to undertake important genetic research."[9]

This concern has encompassed fears of discrimination in many aspects of life, including employment, and health and life insurance. A study on discrimination found that a number of institutions, including health and life insurance companies, health care providers, blood banks, adoption agencies, the military and schools, were reported to have engaged in genetic discrimination against asymptomatic individuals.[10] The discriminatory practices included allegedly treating a genetic diagnosis as a preexisting condition for insurance purposes, refusal by an adoption agency to allow a woman at risk for Huntington's disease to adopt based on the woman's genetic risk, and termination from employment after disclosure of a risk of Huntington's disease.[11] Similarly, another study reported that twenty-two percent of the respondents indicated that they or a family member were refused health insurance as a result of a genetic condition.[12] This study was strongly criticized by the Health Insurance Association of America (HIAA) which has argued that there is no evidence showing that insurers engage in genetic discrimination and that federal legislation to prohibit discrimination based on genetic information is unnecessary.[13] Ronald Adler, President of Laurdan Associates, a human resource management consulting firm, has testified that generally employers do not currently seek employees' genetic information and do not plan to do so. However, he noted that "federal legislation may still be warranted" to help allay fears that may prevent individuals from undergoing potentially life-saving genetic tests or participate in genetic research.[14]

Legal cases of genetic discrimination have been few. However, studies have shown that public fear of discrimination influences the uptake of genetic testing and the use of genetic information by consumers and health professionals. Advisory committees to the Secretary of the U.S. Department of Health and Human Services (HHS) sponsored two public forums to gather perspectives on genetic discrimination. Many comments were received from patients, consumers, health professionals, scientists, genetic test developers, educators, industry representatives, policymakers, lawyers, students and others representing a wide range of diverse ethnic and racial groups.[15] The comments and testimony revealed several anecdotal cases of discrimination. The Secretary's Advisory Committee on Genetic Testing (SACGT) sent two letters to the Secretary of HHS urging support for nondiscrimination protections:

> During consultations with the public SACGT heard from many Americans who are concerned about the misuse of genetic information by third parties, such as health insurers and employers, and the potential for discrimination based on that information. Many stated that fear of genetic discrimination would dissuade them from undergoing a genetic test or participating in genetic research studies. Others stated that they would pay out of pocket for a genetic test to prevent the results from being placed in their medical record. Such concerns are a deterrent to advances in the field of genetic testing and may limit the realization of the benefits of genetic testing.[16]

Similarly, the Secretary's Advisory Committee on Genetics, Health, and Society (SACGHS) recommended that a compilation of testimony from the meeting be prepared and shared with the Secretary of HHS, and Members of Congress. SACGHS indicated that it would work with genetics professional and consumer associations and congressional committees to help move the legislation forward in the 109th Congress.[17]

A joint report by the Department of Labor, the Department of Health and Human Services, the Equal Employment Opportunity Commission and the Department of Justice summarized the various studies on discrimination based on genetic information and argued for the enactment of federal legislation. The report stated that "genetic predisposition or conditions can lead to workplace discrimination, even in cases where workers are healthy and unlikely to develop disease or where the genetic condition has no effect on the ability to perform work" and that "because an individual's genetic information has implications for his or her family members and future generations, misuse of genetic information could have intergenerational effects that are far broader than any individual incident of misuse."[18] Concluding that existing protections are minimal, the report went on to call for the enactment of legislation which states that (1) employers should not require or request that employees or potential employees take a genetic test or provide genetic information as a condition of employment or benefits, (2) employers should not use genetic information to discriminate against, limit, segregate, or classify employees, and (3) employers should not obtain or disclose genetic information about employees or potential employees under most circumstances.[19] According to the Labor Department report, employers should be able to (1) use genetic information for monitoring for the effects of a particular substance in the workplace under certain circumstances, and (2) disclose genetic information for research and other purposes with the written, informed consent of the individuals. In addition, the report states that the statutory authority of federal agencies or contractors to promulgate regulations, enforce workplace safety and health laws, or conduct occupational or other health research should not be limited.[20]

The National Council on Disability (NCD), an independent federal agency that advises the President and Congress on issues affecting individuals with disabilities, published a position paper arguing for the enactment of federal legislation prohibiting genetic discrimination on March 4, 2002. The NCD argues that recent advances in genetic research have brought an increasing potential for genetic discrimination, that genetic discrimination is a historical and current reality, that genetic discrimination undermines the purposes of genetic research and testing, that genetic test information has little value for purposes of making employment decisions and insurance decisions, and that existing laws are insufficient to protect individuals from genetic discrimination.[21]

President Bush has also made the prohibition of genetic discrimination one of the key components of the President's health care reform agenda. The Administration has indicated that it favors enactment of legislation to prohibit the improper use of genetic information in health insurance and employment and supports the enactment of S. 306, 109th Congress.[22] The President had also indicated his support of S. 1053, the Genetic Non-Discrimination Act of 2003, as passed by the Senate October 14, 2003.[23]

It should be emphasized that legal issues relating to genetics may vary depending on whether insurance, employment or other types of discrimination, or medical research are involved. Approaches to addressing the issues raised in these contexts vary from taking no legislative action, addressing certain specific concerns (as was done in the Health Insurance Portability and Accountability Act), or more far reaching approaches such as comprehensive legislation on genetics or legislation focused on all medical records, including genetics.

Generally legal issues raised regarding genetics have been based on two main concepts: privacy and discrimination. The privacy interests of an individual in his or her genetic information have been seen as significant and protecting these interests is seen as making discriminatory actions based on this information less likely. However, another approach would be to prohibit this potential misuse of the information by prohibiting discrimination. Some statutes, like the Americans with Disabilities Act (ADA), 42 U.S.C. §§ 12101 *et seq.*, take a two-pronged approach to similar issues regarding medical information about disabilities by both protecting the confidentiality of the information and by prohibiting discriminatory acts.

Currently there are no federal laws that directly and comprehensively address the issues raised by the use of genetic information. There are, however, a few laws that address parts of these issues but the only federal law that directly addresses the issue of discrimination based on genetic information is the Health Insurance Portability and Accountability Act. On February 8, 2000, President Clinton issued an executive order prohibiting discrimination against federal employees based on protected genetic information. On December 20, 2000, the Department of Health and Human Services issued final regulations on medical privacy which are not specific to genetics but cover all personal health information.[24] This rule went into effect on April 14, 2001 but was amended in 2002.[25] In addition, many states have enacted laws which vary widely in their approaches to genetic information.

THE HEALTH INSURANCE PORTABILITY AND ACCOUNTABILITY ACT OF 1996

P.L. 104-191, the Health Insurance Portability and Accountability Act of 1996[26], has been hailed as taking "important steps toward banning genetic discrimination in health insurance" but has also been criticized as not going far enough.[27] The act prohibits a group health plan or issuer of a group health plan from using genetic information to establish rules for eligibility or continued eligibility and provides that genetic information shall not be treated as a preexisting condition in the absence of the diagnosis of the condition related to such information. It also prohibits a group health plan or issuer of a group health plan from using genetic information in setting a premium contribution. These protections apply to individuals within the group plans; they do not apply to the acceptance of the whole group or to the premiums set for the group. The act would not prohibit group health plans or issuers of plans (i.e., insurers) from requiring or requesting genetic testing, does not require them to obtain authorization before disclosing genetic information, and does not prevent them from excluding all coverage for a particular condition or imposing lifetime caps on all benefits or on specific benefits. In addition, this act does not address the issues of the use of genetic information in contexts other than health insurance such as employment.[28]

EXECUTIVE ORDER

On February 9, 2000, President Clinton signed Executive Order 13145 prohibiting genetic discrimination against employees in federal executive departments and agencies. In announcing the executive order at a meeting of the American Association for the Advancement of Science, the President stated that "This extraordinary march of human understanding imposes on us a profound responsibility to make sure that the age of discovery can continue to reflect our most cherished values."[29] Many commentators lauded the executive order, and quoted with approval its description as "preventive policy making — to put in place the kind of protections that the public needs and deserves before we find ourselves in a needless crisis situation."[30] However, it has also been criticized both on a philosophical level[31] and in the details of its coverage[32] The EEOC has issued guidance on the executive order.[33]

The executive order defines "protected genetic information" as "(A) information about an individual's genetic tests; (B) information about the genetic tests of an individual's family members; or (C) information about the occurrence of a disease; or medical condition or disorder in family members of the individual." Current health status information would not be protected under this executive order unless it was derived from the information described above.

The executive order requires executive departments and agencies to implement the following nondiscrimination requirements:

- the employing entity shall not discharge, fail or refuse to hire, or otherwise discriminate against any employee because of protected genetic information or because of information about a request for or receipt of genetic services;
- the employing entity shall not limit, segregate or classify employees in any way that would deprive or tend to deprive any employee of employment opportunities or otherwise adversely affect that employee's status because of protected genetic information or because of information about a request for or receipt of genetic services;
- the employing entity shall not request, require, collect, or purchase protected genetic information with respect to an employee or information about a request for or receipt of genetic services;
- the employing entity shall not disclose protected genetic information with respect to an employee or information about a request for or receipt of genetic services with certain exceptions;
- the employing entity shall not maintain protected genetic information or information about a request for or receipt of genetic services in general personnel files. Such materials shall be treated as confidential medical records and kept separate from personnel files.

There are certain exceptions to these prohibitions. For example, the employing entity may request or require information if such current condition could prevent the applicant or employee from performing the essential functions of the job, or where it is to be used exclusively to determine whether further medical evaluation is needed to diagnose a current disease. Genetic monitoring of biological effects of toxic substances in the workplaces are permitted in certain circumstances.

THE AMERICANS WITH DISABILITIES ACT

The Americans with Disabilities Act (ADA), 42 U.S.C. § 12101 *et seq.*, prohibits discrimination against an individual with a disability in employment, public services, public accommodations, and communications. The threshold issue in any ADA case is whether the individual alleging discrimination is an individual with a disability. The act defines the term disability with respect to an individual as having "(A) a physical or mental impairment that substantially limits one or more of the major life activities of such individual, (B) a record of such an impairment; or (C) being regarded as having such an impairment."[34] Although the statutory language of the ADA does not reference genetic traits, there was a discussion of the issue during congressional debate.[35] So far there have been no judicial decisions but one case was brought by the EEOC and settled. In addition, Terri Seargent filed with the EEOC alleging genetic discrimination and received a determination on November 21, 2000 that the EEOC's investigation supported her allegation of discrimination under the ADA.[36]

EEOC Interpretation of the ADA Regarding Genetic Discrimination

The ADA has been interpreted by the Equal Employment Opportunity Commission (EEOC) as including genetic information relating to illness, disease, or other disorders.[37] The legislative history was cited by the EEOC in its guidance to the definition of disability for its compliance manual. In this guidance, the EEOC examined the definition of disability under the ADA, noting that the definition was composed of three prongs: disability means (1) a physical or mental impairment that substantially limits one or more of the major life activities of an individual, (2) a record of such an impairment, or (3) being regarded as having such an impairment.[38] It was under the third prong that the EEOC determined that discrimination based on genetic information relating to illness, disease, or other disorders was prohibited.[39]

Although this EEOC interpretation was widely heralded as a significant step for the protection of rights for individuals whose genes indicate an increased susceptibility to illness, disease or other disorders, it is limited in its application and may be even more limited after the recent Supreme Court decisions on the definition of disability.[40] However, the EEOC has not withdrawn this guidance and at recent Senate hearings, EEOC Commissioner Paul Miller stated that the ADA "can be interpreted to prohibit employment discrimination based on genetic information. However, the ADA does not explicitly address the issue and its protections are limited and uncertain." In addition, Commissioner Miller observed that even if the ADA were found to cover genetic discrimination, the requirements of the ADA may not protect workers from all types of genetic discrimination. He stated, "for example, the ADA does not protect workers from requirements or requests to provide genetic information to their employers....In addition, once the applicant is hired, the employer may request that the employee take a medical exam, such as a genetic test, if the employer can demonstrate that the information from that test is job related and consistent with business necessity."[41]

The first ADA case alleging genetic discrimination was filed with the EEOC by Terri Seargent. Ms. Seargent, whose situation was extensively discussed during Senate debate on genetic discrimination in the 106th Congress, had a promising career as a manager for a small insurance broker in North Carolina. She had positive performance evaluations but after medical tests determined that she had Alpha 1 Antitrypson Deficiency, a condition that affects the lungs and liver, and she began taking expensive medication, she was terminated from her employment.[42] Ms. Seargent filed with the EEOC alleging genetic discrimination and received a determination on November 21, 2000 that the EEOC's investigation supported her allegation of discrimination under the ADA.[43]

The EEOC settled its first court action challenging the use of workplace genetic testing under the ADA against Burlington Northern Santa Fe Railway (BNSF). The settlement, announced on April 18, 2001, ended genetic testing of employees who filed claims for work-related injuries based on carpal tunnel syndrome. EEOC Commissioner Paul Steven Miller stated "The Commission will continue to respond aggressively to any evidence that employers are asking for or using genetic tests in a manner that violates the ADA. Employers must understand that basing employment decisions on genetic testing is barred under the ADA's "regarded as" prong, as stated in EEOC's 1995 policy guidance on the definition of the term "disability." Moreover, genetic testing, as conducted in this case, also violates the ADA as an unlawful medical exam."[44]

Supreme Court ADA Decisions

Although the combination of the ADA's legislative history and the EEOC's guidance has led commentators to argue that the ADA would cover genetic discrimination, the merit of these arguments has been uncertain since there have been no reported cases holding that the ADA prohibits genetic discrimination. This uncertainty has increased in light of recent Supreme Court decisions on the ADA.[45]

The first Supreme Court ADA case to address the definition of disability was *Bragdon v. Abbott*, a 1998 case involving a dentist who refused to treat an HIV infected individual outside of a hospital.[46] In *Bragdon,* the Court found that the plaintiff's asymptomatic HIV infection was a physical impairment impacting on the major life activity of reproduction thus rending HIV infection a disability under the ADA. In two 1999 cases the Court examined the definitional issue whether the effects of medication or assistive devices should be taken into consideration in determining whether or not an individual has a disability. The Court in the landmark decisions of *Sutton v. United Airlines[47]* and *Murphy v. United Parcel Service, Inc,[48]* held, contrary to the interpretation given by the EEOC, that the "determination of whether an individual is disabled should be made with reference to measures that mitigate the individual's impairment...."[49] In reaching this holding, the Court looked to the first prong of the definition of disability (having a physical or mental impairment that substantially limits one or more of the major life activities of an individual) and emphasized that the phrase "substantially limits" appears in the present indicative verb form "requiring that a person be presently — not potentially or hypothetically — substantially limited in order to demonstrate a disability." In *Albertsons Inc. v. Kirkingburg[50]* the Court held unanimously that the ADA requires proof that the limitation on a major life activity by the impairment is substantial. The Court in *Sutton* also looked at the findings enacted as part of the ADA which stated that "some 43,000,000 Americans have one or more physical or mental disabilities" and found that this figure was inconsistent with the argument that the statute covered individuals without looking at the mitigating effects of medications or devices. The individualized nature of the inquiry into whether an individual was an individual with a disability was emphasized.

Although the Court's decision in *Sutton* did not turn on the third prong of the definition of disability (being "regarded as having such an impairment") the Court did address the interpretation of this part of the definition. There are two ways, the Court stated, that an individual can fall within the "regarded as" prong: (1) a covered entity mistakenly believes that a person has a physical impairment that substantially limits one or more major life activities, or (2) a covered entity mistakenly believes that an actual impairment substantially limits one or more major life activities. The Court found that, on its own, the allegation that an entity has a vision requirement in place does not establish a claim that the entity regards an individual as substantially impaired in the major life activity of working. The term "substantially limits" was regarded as significant. It requires "at a minimum, that plaintiffs allege they are unable to work in a broad class of jobs." The Court emphasized that it was "assuming without deciding" that working is a major life activity and that the EEOC regulations interpreting "substantially limits" are reasonable and found that even using the EEOC interpretation, the plaintiffs in *Sutton* failed to allege adequately that their vision is regarded as an impairment that substantially limits them in a major life activity. Being precluded from being a global airline pilot was not sufficient since they could obtain other, although less lucrative jobs, as regional pilots or pilot instructors.

The "regarded as" prong was directly at issue in *Murphy*. In *Murphy* the Court held that the fact that an individual with high blood pressure was unable to meet the Department of Transportation (DOT) safety standards was not sufficient to create an issue of fact regarding whether an individual is regarded as unable to utilize a class of jobs. Like *Sutton*, the holding in *Murphy* emphasized the numerous other jobs available to the plaintiff.

The Supreme Court's decisions on the ADA did not directly address genetic discrimination and it is possible that the ADA could be interpreted to cover a particular genetic defect. However, the reasoning used in the Court's recent decisions appears to make it unlikely that an ADA claim based on genetic discrimination would be successful. There are several factors that lead to this conclusion.

First, the Supreme Court in *Sutton* specifically struck down an interpretation by the EEOC regarding the use of mitigating factors and raised questions concerning the validity of the EEOC's interpretation. The Court also found no statutory authority for agency interpretation of the definition of disability. The EEOC had taken the position that whether or not an individual has a disability should be determined by what his or her condition would be without medication or an assistive device. Rejecting this EEOC interpretation, in *Sutton* the Supreme Court noted that no agency was given the authority to interpret the term "disability" but that because both parties accepted the regulations as valid "we have no occasion to consider what deference they are due, if any." Similarly, in *Murphy* the Court clearly stated that its use of the EEOC regulations did not indicate that the regulations were valid. However, in its earlier decision in *Bragdon v. Abbott*, the Court had found its conclusion that HIV infection was covered by the ADA to be "reinforced by administrative guidance issued by the Justice Department...." The cases subsequent to *Bragdon* did not examine this seeming contradiction so exactly how a future decision would view EEOC regulations and guidance is uncertain. This issue is especially important regarding potential cases of genetic discrimination since the EEOC has published guidance indicating that the ADA covers genetic discrimination,[51] and there are no reported cases.

Similarly, the Supreme Court showed little indication to examine the legislative history of the ADA. The Court in *Sutton* held that it was not necessary to consider the legislative history of the ADA regarding the issue of whether individuals should be examined in their uncorrected state or with the use of mitigating medications or devices. It found that the statutory language was sufficient to support its holding on this issue. Although the issue regarding genetic discrimination is distinct from that of the use of mitigating medications and devices, the Court's general reluctance to examine legislative history in *Sutton* may indicate that the language on genetic discrimination quoted above from the congressional debates also would not be examined.

The Court's reliance in *Sutton* upon the findings in the ADA that 43,000,000 Americans have one or more physical disabilities also indicates that the Court may not find genetic defects to be covered. The number of individuals cited in the findings as having a disability was seen by the Court as inconsistent with the argument that the statute covered individuals whose disabilities were mitigated by medications or devices. Since the prevalence of genetic defects is believed to be widespread, coverage of genetic defects could arguably include almost every individual. Thus, it is possible that the Court could use the same rationale as in *Sutton* to find genetic defects not included.

In *Bragdon v. Abbott,* where the Court found that HIV infection was covered under the ADA, the majority opinion spent considerable time discussing the immediate physiological effects of the infection. This would appear to be consistent with the holding in *Sutton* that the "substantially limits" definitional language requires that the substantial limitation not be potential or hypothetical. This reasoning could be contrasted to the situation presented by genetic defects which in many cases do not ever manifest. Interestingly, in his dissenting opinion in *Bragdon v. Abbott,* Chief Justice Rehnquist, who was in the majority in *Sutton*, stated that the argument regarding coverage of HIV infection "taken to its logical extreme, would render every individual with a genetic marker for some debilitating disease 'disabled' here and now because of some possible future effects." Whether the Court would now share the Chief Justice's view that such coverage of genetic discrimination is an invalid interpretation of the definition is uncertain, especially since the Court in *Bragdon* was discussing the first prong of the definition, not the "regarded as" prong which is the most likely basis for coverage of genetic defects.

In its recent cases the Court provided considerable guidance concerning the "regarded as" prong of the definition of disability, the most likely aspect of the definition to be used to find coverage of genetic defects. Including the requirement that the individual be regarded as "substantially limited" in a major life activity, the Court found that this language meant that being precluded from a particular job was not sufficient to be substantially limited in the major life activity of working if other jobs in the same class could be obtained. And when this specific issue was raised in *Murphy*, the plaintiff was not found to be regarded as substantially limited in the major life activity of working. The main point of this rather complicated discussion is that making the case that one is regarded as substantially limited in a major life activity, particularly the major life activity of working, is likely to be difficult.

The Supreme Court's recent decisions do not directly address ADA coverage of genetic discrimination. They emphasize an individualized approach to the determination of whether an individual has a disability under the ADA. Although an argument could be made that the ADA would cover individuals with genetic defects in certain cases, the Court's most recent decisions, particularly *Sutton* and *Murphy*, use reasoning that would make it unlikely that most ADA claims based on genetic discrimination would be successful.[52]

In addition, even assuming the ADA was found to apply, it may not protect employees from having their employers have access to their genetic information. Although the ADA prohibits an employer from making medical inquiries prior to a job offer, the employer may obtain medical information in certain cases after the offer of employment has been made. Assuming that the prohibitions against discrimination in the ADA would apply, it is difficult to prove that genetic information was the reason for discrimination. This raises issues relating to the privacy of genetic information.

Privacy

Although the Constitution does not expressly provide for a right to privacy, the Supreme Court has found some right to informational privacy.[53] However, these rights are limited by judicial deference to government's need to acquire the information and by the fact that such a constitutional right would be limited to state action. As a practical matter, this would mean that federal or state collections of information may receive some constitutional protection but the collection and use of information by private health plans or organizations would not be covered.[54] Certain federal statutes may provide some privacy protection for medical records. The Privacy Act of 1974, 5 U.S.C. § 552a, prohibits the disclosure of records maintained on individuals by federal government agencies except under certain conditions. Subsection 552a(f)(3) allows agencies to establish special procedures for individuals who wish to access their medical records. The intent of this provision as described in the House report was to ensure rules so that an individual who would be adversely affected by the receipt of such data may be apprized of it in a manner which would not cause such adverse effects.[55]

The Freedom of Information Act (FOIA), 5 U.S.C. §§ 552 *et seq.*, establishes a right of access to records maintained by agencies within the executive branch of the federal government. It contains several exemptions, including one for "personnel and medical files and similar files the disclosure of which would constitute a clearly unwarranted invasion of personal privacy."[56] Both the Privacy Act and FOIA may, then, provide some privacy protections for genetic information but they are limited in their scope and would not encompass information held by a private entity.[57]

The ADA provides for some privacy protections for individuals with disabilities in the context of employment. Before an offer of employment is made, an employer may not ask a disability related question or require a medical examination.[58] The EEOC in its guidance on this issue stated that the rationale for this exclusion was to isolate an employer's consideration of an applicant's non-medical qualifications from any consideration of the applicant's medical condition.[59] Once an offer is made, disability related questions and medical examinations are permitted as long as all individuals who have been offered a job in that category are asked the same questions and given the same examinations.[60] The ADA also requires that information obtained regarding medical information be kept in a separate medical file.[61] The precise reach of the protections, especially regarding predictive genetic information is uncertain. As was discussed previously it is not clear whether the definition of disability under the ADA would cover an individual with a genetic predisposition to a condition when that condition has not manifested.[62]

The Health Insurance Portability and Accountability Act (HIPAA) contains requirements for the standardization of electronically transmitted health insurance financial claims and administrative transactions, such as the submission of claims, processing of enrollments, verification of insurance eligibility, and payment and remittance advice. HIPAA required the Secretary of Health and Human Services (HHS) to make recommendations to Congress by August 1997 concerning the protection of privacy of individually identifiable health information and Congress had until August 1999 to enact legislation on this issue. If Congress did not enact legislation, HIPAA requires the Secretary of HHS to promulgate regulations on privacy protections. The Secretary of HHS issued final regulations on December 20, 2000.[63]

The final privacy regulations, which became effective on April 14, 2001, and were modified on August 14, 2002,[64] apply to health insurers, providers, and health care clearinghouses and give patients the right to inspect, copy and in certain situations, amend their medical records. The regulations cover all personal health information in paper, oral or electronic form. Individually identifiable health information is defined broadly and includes genetic information as well as information about an individual's family history.[65] Covered entities are required to have in place reasonable safeguards to protect the privacy of patient information and limit the information used or disclosed to the minimum amount necessary to accomplish the intended purpose of the disclosure. Civil money penalties are provided, although there is no private right of action, and egregious violations carry federal criminal penalties of up to $250,000 and ten years in prison. Although these regulations are general and not specific to genetics, they will have an effect on genetic information. In the comments to the regulations, the Department noted that many commentators requested additional protections for sensitive information, including genetic information. In response, the Department noted that generally the regulations do not differentiate among types of protected health information.[66]

State Statutes

Although there is limited federal law relating to the use of genetic information, many states have enacted statutes dealing with various aspects of these issues. Early state statutes focused on particular genetic conditions. The first statute to prohibit discrimination based on a genetic trait was enacted in North Carolina and prohibited employment discrimination based on the sickle cell trait. In 1991 Wisconsin became the first state to enact a comprehensive law to prohibit discrimination based on genetic test results. Currently, the states vary in their provisions with some prohibiting discrimination in employment while others deal solely with discrimination in insurance. A recent survey of state law found that thirty-two states have enacted genetic nondiscrimination in employment laws.[67] A related survey found that forty-eight states have passed laws pertaining to the use of genetic information in health insurance.[68] One of the most contentious aspects of the state legislation has been the definition of genetic information. Some states, like Michigan, limit nondiscrimination protections to the results of genetic tests. On the other hand, New Jersey prohibits the use of information about genes, gene products or inherited characteristics that may derive from an individual or family member. This would include information such as family history which is often used in insurance underwriting.

Although these state statutes do provide some types of coverage, they do not cover employer self-funded plans providing private health insurance for employees and their dependents. These plans are exempt from state insurance laws due to the preemption provision in the federal Employee Retirement Income Security Act (ERISA).[69] Since it has been estimated that over one-third of the nonelderly insured population obtains its coverage through self-funded plans and these types of plans are increasing, the ERISA exemption limits the application of state laws significantly.[70]

Legislation in the 106th Congress

Although legislation specifically relating to genetic discrimination and privacy was not enacted during the 106th Congress, a provision relating to health insurance was considered in the conference on H.R. 2990. The Senate amended H.R. 2990 as passed by the House, striking all the language after the enacting clause and substituting the language in S. 1344. This Senate bill would have amended ERISA, the Public Health Service Act and the Internal Revenue Code to prohibit health plans or health insurance issuers, in both group and individual markets, from using predictive genetic information to set premiums. It also contained confidentiality provisions.[71]

Senator Daschle had offered a more comprehensive amendment to the FY2001 Labor-HHS Appropriations bill, S. 2553. It would have prohibited insurance companies from raising premiums or denying coverage on the basis of genetic tests and would have also barred employers from using predictive genetic information to make employment-related decisions. The amendment was defeated by a vote of 54-44.

Legislation in the 107th Congress

Legislation relating to genetic discrimination and privacy continued to be a major issue in the 107th Congress. The Senate version of the Patient Protection Act, S. 1052, which passed the Senate on June 29, 2001, contained an amendment prohibiting certain genetic discrimination by group health plans and health insurance issuers. It also contains a provision relating to confidentiality.[72] Congress did not pass the legislation prior to the adjournment of the 107th Congress.

Other Senate legislation in the 107th took various approaches. S. 318, introduced by Senator Daschle, would have prohibited genetic nondiscrimination in health insurance and employment. S. 1995 sponsored by Senators Snowe, Frist and Jeffords, also would have prohibited genetic discrimination in insurance and employment but was less broad that S. 318. S. 19, the Protecting Civil Rights for all Americans Act introduced by Senator Daschle, contained nondiscrimination provisions relating to insurance and employment. Senator Snowe also introduced S. 382, the Genetic Information Nondiscrimination in Health Insurance Act of 2001, which would have prohibited discrimination in insurance. S. 450, the Financial Institution Privacy Protection Act of 2001 introduced by Senator Nelson, contained provisions protection the privacy of health information, including genetic information.[73]

In the House, Representative Slaughter introduced H.R. 602, the Genetic Nondiscrimination in Health Insurance and Employment Act, which would have prohibited genetic discrimination in insurance and employment. H.R. 602 was paralleled by S. 318 in the Senate.

Legislation in the 108th Congress

Legislation relating to genetic discrimination and privacy continued to be a major issue in the 108th Congress. Several bills were introduced to address genetic discrimination and privacy. For example, S. 16, the Equal Rights and Equal Dignity for Americans Act of 2003 introduced by Senator Daschle on January 17, 2003, contained nondiscrimination provisions relating to insurance and employment. On May 1, 2003, Representative Slaughter introduced H.R. 1910, The Genetic Nondiscrimination in Health Insurance and Employment Act, which prohibited genetic discrimination in insurance and employment. H.R. 1910 was a companion to S. 1053, introduced by Senator Snowe on May 13, 2003, in the Senate.

On October 14, 2003, the Senate passed the Genetic Information Nondiscrimination Act of 2003 (S. 1053).[74] This bill prohibited health insurance plans from denying enrollment or charging higher premiums to individuals based on the individual's or family member's genetic information. In addition, the bill banned the collection, use and disclosure of genetic information for insurance underwriting purposes. In the employment context, this bill prohibited the use of genetic information in employment decisions, such as hiring, firing, job assignments and promotions. The bill also prevented the acquisition and disclosure of genetic information as well as applies the procedures and remedies authorized under the Civil Rights Act of 1964 to cases of genetic discrimination. Although President Bush supported genetic discrimination legislation and the House held a hearing in July 2004,[75] the House did not pass a bill in the 108th Congress.

Legislation in the 109th Congress

In the 109th Congress, S. 306, the Genetic Information Nondiscrimination Act of 2005, was introduced by Senator Snowe on February 7, 2005. The Senate Health, Education, Labor and Pensions Committee reported S. 306 out with an amendment in the nature of a substitute by a voice vote. The bill was passed, with an amendment, on February 17, 2005 by a vote of 98-0. The amendment deleted former section 103 which would have added a prohibition of discrimination based on genetic information or services in church health insurance plans to the Internal Revenue Code. This section may be added by the House or in conference. The Administration has indicated that it favors enactment of legislation to prohibit the improper use of genetic information in health insurance and employment and supports the enactment of S. 306, 109th Congress.[76] A companion bill, H.R. 1227, was introduced in the House on March 10, 2004 by Representative Biggert. H.R. 1227 was referred to the House Committees on Education and the Workforce, Energy and Commerce, and Ways and Means.

S. 306 is similar to S. 1053, which passed the Senate in 2003. It prohibits health insurance plans from denying enrollment or charging higher premiums to individuals based on the individual's or family member's genetic information. In addition, it contains privacy provisions prohibiting certain uses and disclosures of genetic information as well as prohibiting the collection of genetic information for insurance underwriting purposes. S. 306 also prohibits discrimination in employment because of genetic information and, with certain exceptions, prohibits an employer from requesting, requiring, or purchasing genetic information. If such information is obtained, the bill requires that it be treated as part of a confidential medical record. There are detailed provisions on enforcement which generally apply the remedies available in existing civil rights laws such as Title VII of the Civil Rights Act of 1964, 42 U.S.C. § 2000e-4 *et seq.*

References

[1] The Human Genome Project, begun in 1990, is a 13 year effort coordinated by the U.S. Department of Energy and the National Institutes of Health to identify all of the protein-coding genes in human DNA and to determine the sequences of the 3 billion chemical bases that make up human DNA, store this information in data bases, develop tools for data analysis, and address the ethical, legal, and social issues (ELSI) that may arise from the project. The Human Genome Project is funded through the Department of Energy and the National Institutes of Health. For more detailed information see "The National Human Genome Research Institute," [http://www.genome.gov/], and "Human Genome Research," [http://www.er.doe.gov/production/ober/hug_top.html]

[2] "International Human Genome Sequencing Consortium Describes Finished Human Genome Sequence, October, 20, 2004, at [http://www.genome.gov/12513430]. Accessed January 5, 2005.

[3] Testimony of Francis S. Collins, Director, National Human Genome Research Institute, National Institutes of Health, Before the Senate Health, Education, Labor and Pensions Committee (July 20, 2000).

[4] For more information on the status of genetic tests and further discussion of what constitutes 'genetic information', see CRS Report RL32478, "Genetic Testing: Scientific Background and Nondiscrimination Legislation," July 20, 2004, by Michele Schoonmaker and Erin Williams.

[5] Rick Weiss, "Genetic Therapy Apparently Cures 2," The Washington Post A-1 (April 28, 2000).

[6] Testimony of Bill Frist United States Senator Tennessee Before the Senate Committee on Health, Education, Labor and Pensions Subcommittee on Public Health, Gene Therapy: Is there Oversight for Patient Safety?" (February 2, 2000).

[7] The group working on these issues is referred to as the Ethical, Legal and Social Implications (ELSI) program. See [http://www.genome.gov/page.cfm?pageID=10001618].

[8] Testimony by Dr. Francis Collins, Director, National Center for Human Genome Research, Before the Senate Committee on Labor and Human Resources (March 6, 1996). See also, Hudson, Rothenberg, Andrews, Kahn, and Collins, "Genetic Discrimination and Health Insurance: An Urgent Need for Reform," 270 Science 391 (Oct. 20, 1995); Annas, Glantz and Roche, "Drafting the Genetic Privacy Act: Science, Policy and Practical Considerations," 23 J. of Law, Medicine and Ethics 360 (1995); Gostin, "Genetic Discrimination: The Use of Genetically Based Diagnostic and Prognostic Tests by Employers and Insurers," 17 Am. J. of Law and Med. 109 (1991); Rothstein, Mark, Genetic Secrets: Protecting Privacy and Confidentiality in the Genetic Era (1997).

[9] Testimony of Francis S. Collins, Director, National Human Genome Research Institute, National Institutes of Health, Before the Senate Health, Education, Labor and Pensions Committee (July 20, 2000).

[10] Geller, Alper, Billings, Barash, Beckwith, and Natowicz, "Individual, Family, and Societal Dimensions of Genetic Discrimination: A Case Study Analysis," 2 Science and Engineering Ethics 71 (1996). The study has been criticized by the insurance industry

as relying on anecdotal information. See American Council of Life Insurance, "Statement Regarding the Council for Responsible Genetics 'Study' on Genetic Discrimination" (April 11, 1996).

[11] Id.

[12] Lapham, E. Virginia, Kozma, Chahira, Weiss, Joan O., "Genetic Discrimination: Perspectives of Consumers," 274 Science 621 (October 25, 1996).

[13] "Testimony of the HIAA on Genetic Testing," Before the Senate Committee on Labor and Human Resources, 105th Cong., 2d Sess. (May 21, 1998).

[14] "Testimony of Ronald L. Adler, President of Laurdan Associates, Inc.,"Protecting Against Genetic Discrimination: The Limits of Existing Laws," Before the Senate Committee on Health, Education, Labor and Pensions, 107th Cong., 2d Sess. (Feb. 13, 2002), reprinted at [http://help.senate.gov/Hearings-2002/feb2002/021302wit/Adler.pdf].

[15] Highlights and transcripts of January 27, 2000 testimony can be found on the SACGT website at [http://www4.od.nih.gov/oba/sacgt/sacgtmtg.htm], Transcripts of the October 18, 2004 testimony can be found on the SACGHS website at [http://www4.od.nih.gov/oba/SACGHS/meetings/October2004/SACGHSOct2004postmeeting.htm].

[16] From a letter from SACGT to Secretary Tommy Thompson, May 3, 2001, at [http://www4.od.nih.gov/oba/sacgt/ltr_to_secDHHS5-3-01.pdf].

[17] Testimony of Dr. Reed Tuckson, Chair, Secretary's Advisory Committee on Genetics, Health and Society, "Next Steps and Closing Remarks," October 19, 2004, at [http://www4.od.nih.gov/oba/SACGHS/meetings/October2004/transcript/Next_Steps_Cl osing_Remarks_trans.pdf].

[18] Department of Labor, Department of Health and Human Services, Equal Employment Opportunity Commission, Department of Justice, "Genetic Information and the Workplace," [http://www.dol.gov/asp/programs/history/herman/reports/genetics.htm] 2-3 (January 20, 1998).

[19] Department of Labor, Department of Health and Human Services, Equal Employment Opportunity Commission, Department of Justice, "Genetic Information and the Workplace," [http://www.dol.gov/asp/programs/history/herman/reports/genetics.htm] at 7 (January 20, 1998).

[20] Id.

[21] National Council on Disability, "Position Paper on Genetic Discrimination Legislation" [http://www.ncd.gov/newsroom/publications/2002/geneticdiscrimination_principles.htm]

[22] "Statement of Administration Policy, S. 306– Genetic Information Nondiscrimination Act of 2005," reprinted in 151 Cong. Rec. S. 1481 (Daily ed. Feb 16, 2005).

[23] Executive Office of the President, Office of Management and Budget, "Statement of Administrative Policy: S. 1053 — Genetic Non-Discrimination Act of 2003," October 14, 2003, at [http://www.whitehouse.gov/omb/legislative/sap//108-1/s1053sap-s.pdf].

[24] 65 Fed. Reg. 82460 (Dec. 20, 2000).

[25] See *infra* pp. 14-16 for a more detailed discussion.

[26] For a general discussion of this act see, Hinda R. Chaikind, Jean Hearne, Bob Lyke, and Stephen Redhead, *The Health Insurance Portability and Accountability Act (HIPAA) of 1996: Overview and Guidance on Frequently Asked Questions,* CRS Report RL31634.

[27] Statement of Rep. Louise Slaughter Before the House Science Subcommittee on Technology, Hearing on Technological Advance in Genetic Testing: Implications for the Future, September 17, 1996.

[28] It should also be noted the HIPAA contains certain requirements regarding the standardization of claims that raise potential privacy issues. HIPAA addressed these issues by requiring either congressional action or regulatory action to protect privacy. A more detailed discussion of this issue is contained in the section on privacy.

[29] "President's Order Bars Discrimination Based on Genetics," Investor's Business Daily A9 (February 9, 2000).

[30] Wendy R. Uhlmann, "When Genes are Decoded, Who Should See the Results?; Every one of us at Risk," The New York Times F7 (February 29, 2000).

[31] Michael Kinsley, editor of Slate, an online magazine, observed that "genetic discrimination is universal, inevitable and, in some ways, essential....Practice, practice will get you to Carnegie Hall, but only if you've been born on the right bus....The world would be a poorer place if it did not distinguish between me and Yo-Yo Ma in doling out opportunities to be a concert cellist." Michael Kinsley, "Genetic Correctness," The Washington Post A29 (April 18, 2000).

[32] Mark A. Hall, a law professor at Wake Forest University, argues that the order's prohibition of considering predictive genetic information would not allow for the screening of susceptibility to toxic exposure prior to working in such an environment and would not allow for the use of genetic predispositions to future conditions that could effect job performance. Mark A. Hall, "When Genes are Decoded, Who Should See the Results?; Many 'Greatly Overestimate the Risk'," The Washington Post F7 (February 29, 2000).

[33] [http://www.eeoc.gov/policy/docs/guidance-genetic.html]

[34] 42 U.S.C. §12102.

[35] Rep. Owens stated that "[t]hese protections of the ADA will also benefit individuals who are identified through genetic tests as being carriers of a disease-associated gene. There is a record of genetic discrimination against such individuals, most recently during sickle cell screening programs in the 1970's. With the advent of new forms of genetic testing, it is even more critical that the protections of the ADA be in place. Under the ADA, such individuals may not be discriminated against simply because they may not be qualified for a job sometime in the future. The determination as to whether an individual is qualified must take place at the time of the employment decision, and may not be based on speculation regarding the future. Moreover, such individuals may not be discriminated against because they or their children might incur increased health care costs for the employer." 136 Cong. Rec. H 4623 (daily ed. July 12, 1990) (remarks of Rep. Owens). Similarly, Rep. Edwards and Rep. Waxman also stated that individuals who are carriers of a disease-associated gene may not be discriminated against under the ADA. 136 Cong. Rec. H 4625 (daily ed. July 12, 1990) (Statement of Rep. Edwards); Id. at H 4627 (Statement of Rep. Waxman).

[36] Testimony of Janiori Goldman before the House Committee on Energy and Commerce, Subcommittee on Health, 107th Cong., 1st Sess. (March 22, 2001).

[37] Equal Employment Opportunity Commission, Compliance Manual, vol. 2, section 902, order 915.002,902-45 (1995). It is also possible that title VII of the Civil Rights Act of 1964, 42 U.S.C. § 2000e et seq.,may provide some protection against certain kinds of

genetic discrimination since an argument could be made that discrimination based on genetic disorders that are racially or ethnically based, such as sickle cell disease, is prohibited under title VII. However, there are relatively few genetic conditions that have a strong connection with a racial or ethnic group, thus limiting the scope of potential coverage.

[38] 42 U.S.C. §12102(2).

[39] The EEOC gave the following example of its application of the third prong of the definition to genetic discrimination. CP's genetic profile reveals an increased susceptibility to colon cancer. CP is currently asymptomatic and may never in fact develop colon cancer. After making CP a conditional offer of employment, R learns about CP's increased susceptibility to colon cancer. R then withdraws the job offer because of concerns about matters such as CP's productivity, insurance costs and attendance. R is treating CP as having an impairment that substantially limits a major life activity. Accordingly CP is covered by the third part of the definition of disability.

[40] Prior to the Supreme Court's decisions there were three major limitations on the EEOC interpretation. First, the ADA specifically excludes insurance from its coverage except that this exclusion "shall not be used as a subterfuge to evade the purposes of title I and III." The exact parameters of this provision, especially as it relates to genetic information, are unclear although it would appear fair to say the nondiscrimination protections for individuals with certain genes would be considerably stronger in the employment context than when such individuals are being considered for insurance coverage. Second, the EEOC interpretation is part of guidance issued in its compliance manual. Specific prohibitions of discrimination in this area were not included in the statute and were also not part of the EEOC's regulations. Even if a court gives deference to the guidance as indicative of the agency's view of the statute, a court would not likely give such guidance the deference it would accord to statutory or regulatory language. In addition, even assuming the ADA was found to apply, it may not protect employees from having their employers have access to their genetic information. Although the ADA prohibits an employer from making medical inquiries prior to a job offer, the employer may obtain medical information in certain cases after the offer of employment has been made. Even if the prohibitions against discrimination in the ADA would apply, it would be difficult to prove that genetic information was the reason for discrimination. This raises issues relating to the privacy of genetic information which are beyond the scope of this memorandum.

[41] Statement of Commissioner Paul Steven Miller, U.S. Equal Employment Opportunity Commission, Before the Senate Committee on Health, Education, Labor and Pensions (July 20, 2000.

[42] 146 Cong. Rec. S6050 (daily ed. June 29, 2000)(remarks of Sen. Kennedy).

[43] Testimony of Janiori Goldman before the House Committee on Energy and Commerce, Subcommittee on Health, 107th Cong., 1st Sess. (March 22, 2001).

[44] [http://www.eeoc.gov/press/4-18-01.html].

[45] For a discussion of the Supreme Court's ADA decisions see CRS Report RL31401, *The Americans with Disabilities Act: Supreme Court Decisions.*

[46] 524 U.S. 624 (1998). For a more detailed discussion of this decision see CRS Report 98-599, *The Americans with Disabilities Act: HIV Infection is Covered Under the Act.*

[47] 527 U.S. 471 (1999).

[48] 527 U.S. 516 (1999).

[49] *Sutton v. United Airlines*. See also *Murphy v. United Parcel Service*, where the Court held that the determination of whether the petitioner's high blood pressure substantially limits one or more major life activities must be made considering the mitigating measures he employs.

[50] 527 U.S. 555 (1999).

[51] EEOC Compliance Manual, Vol. 2, section 902, order 915.002,902-45 (1995).

[52] In testimony before the Senate Committee on Health, Education, Labor and Pensions, Andrew J. Imparato, the President and CEO of the American Association of People with Disabilities testified that "the ADA as drafted does provide some protections against genetic discrimination in employment, but the law has been interpreted by the Supreme Court and lower federal courts in a manner which weakens its protections. Whereas the ADA can be and has been used to stop genetic discrimination in some instances, the protections it affords offer little security to people with genetic markers and health conditions that have not yet developed into full-blown debilitating conditions." Testimony of Andrew J. Imparato, "Protecting Against Genetic Discrimination: The Limits of Existing Laws," Before the Senate Committee on Health, Education, Labor and Pensions, 107th Cong., 2d Sess. (Feb. 13, 2002), reprinted at [http://help.senate.gov/Hearings-2002/feb2002/021302wit/Imparato.pdf]

[53] See e.g., *Whalen v. Roe*, 429 U.S. 589 (1977).

[54] For a more detailed discussion of this issue see Gostin, "Genetic Privacy," 23 J. of Law, Medicine and Ethics 320 (1995).

[55] H.Rept. 93-1416. 93d Cong., 2d Sess. 16-17 (1974).

[56] 5 U.S.C. §552(b)(6).

[57] For a discussion of recent developments in medical records privacy see CRS Report RS20500, *Medical Records Privacy: Questions and Answers on the HIPAA Final Rule.*

[58] 42 U.S.C. §12112.

[59] EEOC, "ADA Enforcement Guidance: Preemployment Disability-Related Questions and Medical Examinations," Oct. 10, 1995.

[60] Id.

[61] 42 U.S.C. §12112(d)(3) and (4).

[62] One commentator has observed that "the complexity of the ADA, its differential treatment of prospective and existing employees, the especially wide latitude that employers have to require medical examinations and make medical inquiries at the post-offer stage and the centrality of the concept of 'disability' to the operation of the statute have led to confusion in the courts, and in many workplaces, about the precise contours of the ADA's privacy protections." Joanne L. Hustead and Janlori Goldman, "The Genetics Revolution: Conflicts, Challenges, and Conundra: Genetics and Privacy," 28 Am. J. L. and Med. 285, 294 (2002).

[63] 65 Fed. Reg. 82461 (Dec. 20, 2000). For a more detailed discussion, see CRS Report RS20500, *Medical Records Privacy: Questions and Answers on the HIPAA Final Rule*, and CRS Report RS20934, *A Brief Summary of the Medical Privacy Rule.*

[64] 67 Fed. Reg. 53181 (Aug. 14, 2002).

[65] There are additional protections regarding "psychotherapy notes."

[66] 65 Fed. Reg. 82731 (Dec. 20, 2000). A hearing in the 107th Congress examined the issues relating to the privacy of genetic information. See "Privacy Concerns Raised by

the Collection and Use of Genetic Information by Employers and Insurers" Before the House Subcommittee on the Constitution of the House Judiciary Committee, 107th Cong., 2d Sess. (September 12, 2002).

[67] National Conference of State Legislatures Genetics Tables, State Genetics Employment Laws, [http://www.ncsl.org/programs/health/genetics/ndiscrim.htm]. See also, "Genetic Information and the Workpl ace: Enacted Legislation," [http://www.nhgri.nih.gov/Policy_and_public_affairs/Legislation/workplace.htm].

[68] National Conference of State Legislatures Genetics Tables, State Genetic Nondiscrimination in Health Insurance, [http://www.ncsl.org/programs/health/genetics/ndishlth.htm].

[69] 29 U.S.C. §§ 1001-1145.

[70] Hudson, "Genetic Discrimination and Health Insurance: an Urgent Need for Reform," 270 Science 391 (1995); Rothenberg, "Genetic Information and Health Insurance: State Legislative Approaches," 23 J. of Law, Med. and Ethics 312 (1995).

[71] For a more detailed discussion, see CRS Report RL30144, Side-by-Side Comparison of H.R. 2990 and the Senate Amendment for Patient Protection.

[72] For a more detailed discussion of the Patient Protection Legislation, see CRS Report RL31631, *Patient Protection and Managed Care*.

[73] For a more detailed discussion of this legislation, see CRS Report RS20185, *Privacy Protection for Customer Financial Information*.

[74] 149 Cong. Rec S12394-12508 (daily ed. Oct. 4, 2003).

[75] "Genetic Non-Discrimination: Examining the Implications for Workers and Employers" Subcommittee on Employer-Employee Relations, House Committee on Education and Workforce (July 22, 2004).

[76] "Statement of Administration Policy, S. 306– Genetic Information Nondiscrimination Act of 2005," reprinted in 151 Cong. Rec. S. 1481 (Daily ed. Feb 16, 2005).

In: Genetic Discrimination
Editor: Leana J. Albertson, pp. 61-85
ISBN: 978-1-60456-357-3

Chapter 4

GENETIC NON-DISCRIMINATION IN EMPLOYMENT: A COMPARISON OF TITLE II PROVISIONS IN S. 358 AND H.R. 493, 110TH CONGRESS*

Nancy Lee Jones

ABSTRACT

H.R. 493, 110th Congress, the Genetic Information Nondiscrimination Act (GINA), passed the House on April 25, 2007. The Senate bill, S. 358, 110th Congress, was reported out of the Senate Health, Education, Labor, and Pensions Committee on March 29, 2007, and is currently awaiting Senate action. This report compares the provisions of H.R. 493 and S. 358 relating to GINA's prohibition of genetic discrimination in employment.

INTRODUCTION

H.R. 493, 110th Congress, the Genetic Information Nondiscrimination Act (GINA), passed the House on April 25, 2007. The Senate bill, S. 358, 110th Congress, was reported out of the Senate Health, Education, Labor, and Pensions Committee on March 29, 2007, and is currently awaiting Senate action. This report compares the provisions of H.R. 493 and S. 358 relating to GINA's prohibition of genetic discrimination in employment.[1]

OVERVIEW OF DIFFERENCES IN S. 358 AND H.R. 493

Both the House and Senate versions of GINA prohibit discrimination in employment because of genetic information and, with certain exceptions, prohibit an employer from requesting, requiring, or purchasing genetic information. The House and Senate versions of

* Excerpted from CRS Report RL33987, dated May 2, 2007.

GINA are similar in many respects; however, there are several significant differences. For example, the employment sections of the bills contain differing versions of the definitions of "family member"[2] and "genetic information."[3] Generally, where the employment provisions describe unlawful employment practices, S. 358 includes a prohibition against discrimination on the basis of "information about a request for or the receipt of genetic services by such employee or family member of such employee,"[4] whereas the House version does not explicitly include this prohibition. The House bill contains an exception to the prohibition of discrimination regarding DNA analysis for law enforcement purposes,[5] which does not have a parallel provision in the Senate bill.

Section 206 of both S. 358 and H.R. 493 provides for the treatment of genetic information as part of a confidential medical record. The House bill, but not the Senate bill, provides that an employer, employment agency, labor organization, or joint labor-management committee "shall be considered to be in compliance with the maintenance of information requirements of this subsection with respect to genetic information subject to this subsection that is maintained with and treated as a confidential medical record under section 102(d)(3)(B) of the Americans with Disabilities Act..."[6] The House bill, but not the Senate bill, also contains a provision relating to the Health Insurance Portability and Accountability Act (HIPAA) stating: "this title does not prohibit a covered entity under such regulations from any use or disclosure of health information that is authorized for the covered entity under such regulations. The previous sentence does not affect the authority of such Secretary to modify such regulations."[7]

H.R. 493, but not S. 358, adds a provision relating to the genetic information of a fetus or embryo. The House bill provides that references to genetic information include genetic information on a fetus carried by a pregnant woman and, with respect to an individual utilizing assisted reproductive technology, includes genetic information of any embryo legally held by the individual or family member.[8]

Table 1. Prohibiting Employment Discrimination on the Basis of Genetic Information (Title II)

	S. 358 (as reported by the HELP Committee, March 29, 2007)	H.R. 493 (as passed by the House, April 25, 2007)
Section 201(1)	(1) COMMISSION- The term "Commission" means the Equal Employment Opportunity Commission as created by section 705 of the Civil Rights Act of 1964 (42 U.S.C. 2000e-4).	Same as Senate subsection 201(1).
Section 201(2)(A)	(A) IN GENERAL- The term "employee" means —(i) an employee (including an applicant), as defined in section 701(f) of the Civil Rights Act of 1964 (42 U.S.C. 2000e(f)); (ii) a State employee (including an applicant) described in section 304(a) of the Government Employee Rights Act of 1991 (42 U.S.C. 2000e-16c(a)); (iii) a covered employee (including an applicant), as defined in section 101 of the Congressional Accountability Act of 1995 (2 U.S.C. 1301); (iv) a covered employee (including an applicant), as defined in section 411(c) of title 3, United States Code; or (v) an employee or applicant to which section 717(a) of the Civil Rights Act of 1964 (42 U.S.C. 2000e-16(a)) applies.	Same as Senate subsection 201(2)(A).
Section 201(2)(B)	(B) EMPLOYER- The term "employer" means — (i) an employer (as defined in section 701(b) of the Civil Rights Act of 1964 (42 U.S.C. 2000e(b)); (ii) an entity employing a State employee described in section 304(a) of the Government Employee Rights Act of 1991; (iii) an employing office, as defined in section 101 of the Congressional Accountability Act of 1995; (iv) an employing office, as defined in section 411(c) of title 3 , United States Code; or (v) an entity to which section 717(a) of the Civil Rights Act of 1964 applies.	Same as Senate subsection 201(2)(B).
Section 201(2)(C-D)	(C) EMPLOYMENT AGENCY; LABOR ORGANIZATION- The terms "employment agency" and "labor organization" have the meanings given the terms in section 701 of the Civil Rights Act of 1964 (42 U.S.C. 2000e). (D) MEMBER- The term "member," with respect to a labor organization, includes an applicant for membership in a labor organization.	Same as Senate subsections 201(2)(C-D).

Table 1. (Continued).

	S. 358 (as reported by the HELP Committee, March 29, 2007)	H.R. 493 (as passed by the House, April 25, 2007)
Section 201(3)	(3) Family Member. — The term "family member" means with respect to an individual — (A) the spouse of the individual; (B) a dependent child of the individual, including a child who is born to or placed for adoption with the individual; and (C) all other individuals related by blood to the individual or the spouse or child described in subparagraph (A) or (B).	(3) Family Member. — The term "family member" means with respect to an individual —(A)a dependent (as such term is used for purposes of section 701(f)(2) of the Employee Retirement Income Security Act of 1974) of such individual; and (B) any other individual who is a first-degree, seconddegree, third-degree, or fourth-degree relative of an individual described in subparagraph (A).
Section 201(4)	(4) Genetic Information. — (A) In general. — Except as provided in subparagraph (B), the term "genetic information" means information about — (i) an individual's genetic tests (ii) the genetic tests of family members of the individual; or (iii) the occurrence of a disease or disorder in family members of the individual. (B) Exceptions. — The term "genetic information" shall not include information about the sex or age of an individual.	(4) Genetic Information. — (A) In general. — The term "genetic information" means, with respect to any individual, information about — (i) such individual's genetic tests; (ii) the genetic tests of family members of such individual; and (iii) subject to subparagraph (D), the manifestation of a disease or disorder in family members of such individual. (B) Inclusion of Genetic Services. — Such term includes, with respect to any individual, any request for, or receipt of, genetic services (including genetic services received pursuant to participation in clinical research) by such individual or any family member of such individual. (C) Exclusions. — The term "genetic information" shall not include information about the sex or age of any individual.
Section 201(5)	(5) GENETIC MONITORING- The term "genetic monitoring" means the periodic examination of employees to evaluate acquired modifications to their genetic material, such as chromosomal damage or evidence of increased occurrence of mutations, that may have developed in the course of employment due to exposure to toxic substances in the workplace, in order to identify, evaluate, and respond to the effects of or control adverse environmental exposures in the workplace.	Same as Senate subsections 201(5).

Section 201(6)	(6) GENETIC SERVICES- The term "genetic services" means — (A) a genetic test; (B) genetic counseling (such as obtaining, interpreting or assessing genetic information); or (C) genetic education.	(6) GENETIC SERVICES- The term "genetic services" means — (A) a genetic test; (B) genetic counseling (including obtaining, interpreting, or assessing genetic information); or (C) genetic education.
Section 201(7)	(7) GENETIC TEST- (A) IN GENERAL- The term "genetic test" means the analysis of human DNA, RNA, chromosomes, proteins, or metabolites, that detects genotypes, mutations, or chromosomal changes. (B) EXCEPTION- The term "genetic test" does not mean an analysis of proteins or metabolites that does not detect genotypes, mutations, or chromosomal changes.	(7) GENETIC TEST- (A) IN GENERAL- The term "genetic test" means an analysis of human DNA, RNA, chromosomes, proteins, or metabolites, that detects genotypes, mutations, or chromosomal changes. (B) EXCEPTIONS- The term "genetic test" does not mean an analysis of proteins or metabolites that does not detect genotypes, mutations, or chromosomal changes.
Section 202(a)	(a) Use of Genetic Information. — It shall be an unlawful employment practice for an employer — (1) to fail or refuse to hire or to discharge any employee, or otherwise to discriminate against any employee with respect to the compensation, terms, conditions, or privileges of employment of the employee, because of genetic information with respect to the employee (or information about a request for or the receipt of genetic services by such employee or family member of such employee); or (2) to limit, segregate, or classify the employees of the employer in any way that would deprive or tend to deprive any employee of employment opportunities or otherwise adversely affect the status of the employee as an employee, because of genetic information with respect to the employee (or information about a request for or the receipt of genetic services by such employee or family member of such employee).	(a) Discrimination Based on Genetic Information. — It shall be an unlawful employment practice for an employer — (1) to fail or refuse to hire or to discharge any employee, or otherwise to discriminate against any employee with respect to the compensation, terms, conditions, or privileges of employment of the employee, because of genetic information with respect to the employee or (2) to limit, segregate, or classify the employees of the employer in any way that would deprive or tend to deprive any employee of employment opportunities or otherwise adversely affect the status of the employee as an employee, because of genetic information with respect to the employee.

Table 1. (Continued).

	S. 358 (as reported by the HELP Committee, March 29, 2007)	H.R. 493 (as passed by the House, April 25, 2007)
Section 202(b)	(b)Acquisition of Genetic Information. — It shall be an unlawful employment practice for an employer to request, require, or purchase genetic information with respect to an employee or a family member of the employee (or information about a request for the receipt of genetic services by such employee or a family member of such employee) except —	(b)Acquisition of Genetic Information. — It shall be an unlawful employment practice for an employer to request, require, or purchase genetic information with respect to an employee or a family member of the employee except —
Section 202(b)(1)-(2)	(1) where an employer inadvertently requests or requires family medical history of the employee or family member of the employee; (2) where — (A) health or genetic services are offered by the employer, including such services offered as part of a bona fide wellness program; (B) the employee provides prior, knowing, voluntary, and written authorization; (C) only the employee (or family member if the family member is receiving genetic services) and the licensed health care professional or board certified genetic counselor involved in providing such services receive individually identifiable information concerning the results of such services; and (D) any individually identifiable genetic information provided under subparagraph (C) in connection with the services provided under subparagraph (A) is only available for purposes of such services and shall not be disclosed to the employer except in aggregate terms that do not disclose the identity of specific employees;	Same as Senate subsections 202(b)(1)-(2).
Section 202(b)(3)-(4)	(3) where an employer requests or requires family medical history from the employee to comply with the certification provisions of section 103 of the Family and Medical Leave Act of 1993 (29 U.S.C. 2613) or such requirements under State family and medical leave laws; (4) where an employer purchases documents that are commercially and publicly available (including newspapers, magazines, periodicals, and books, but not including medical databases or court records) that include family medical history; or	Same as Senate subsections 202(b)(3)-(4).

Section 202(b)(5)(A)-(D)	(5) where the information involved is to be used for genetic monitoring of the biological effects of toxic substances in the workplace, but only if — (A) the employer provides written notice of the genetic monitoring to the employee; (B)(i) the employee provides prior, knowing, voluntary, and written authorization; or (ii) the genetic monitoring is required by Federal or State law; (C) the employee is informed of individual monitoring results; (D) the monitoring is in compliance with — (i) any Federal genetic monitoring regulations, including any such regulations that may be promulgated by the Secretary of Labor pursuant to the Occupational Safety and Health Act of 1970 (29 U.S.C. 651 et seq.), the Federal Mine Safety and Health Act of 1977 (30 U.S.C. 801 et seq.), or the Atomic Energy Act of 1954 (42 U.S.C. 2011 et seq.); or (ii) State genetic monitoring regulations, in the case of a State that is implementing genetic monitoring regulations under the authority of the Occupational Safety and Health Act of 1970 (29 U.S.C. 651 et seq.); and	Same as Senate subsection 202(b)(5) except the word "or" is added at the end of the subsection.
Section 202(b)(5)(E)	(E) the employer, excluding any licensed health care professional or board certified genetic counselor that is involved in the genetic monitoring program, receives the results of the monitoring only in aggregate terms that do not disclose the identity of specific employees;	Same as Senate subsection 202(b)(5) except the word "or" is added at the end of the subsection.
Section 202(b)(6)	No comparable provision	(6) where the employer conducts DNA analysis for law enforcement purposes as a forensic laboratory, includes such analysis in the Combined DNA Index System pursuant to section 210304 of the Violent Crime Control and Law Enforcement Act of 1994 (42 U.S.C. 14132), and requests or requires genetic information of such employer's employees, but only to the extent that such genetic information is used for analysis of DNA identification markers for quality control to detect sample contamination.
Section 202(c)	(c) Preservation of Protections. — In the case of information to which any of paragraphs (1) through (5) of subsection (b) applies, such information may not be used in violation of paragraph (1) or (2) of subsection (a) or treated or disclosed in a manner that violates section 206.	(c) Preservation of Protections. — In the case of information to which any of paragraphs (1) through (6) of subsection (b) applies, such information may not be used in violation of paragraph (1) or (2) of subsection (a) or treated or disclosed in a manner that violates section 206.

Table 1. (Continued).

	S. 358 (as reported by the HELP Committee, March 29, 2007)	H.R. 493 (as passed by the House, April 25, 2007)
Section 203(a)	(a) Use of Genetic Information- It shall be an unlawful employment practice for an employment agency — (1) to fail or refuse to refer for employment, or otherwise to discriminate against, any individual because of genetic information with respect to the individual (or information about a request for or the receipt of genetic services by such individual or family member of such individual); (2) to limit, segregate, or classify individuals or fail or refuse to refer for employment any individual in any way that would deprive or tend to deprive any individual of employment opportunities, or otherwise adversely affect the status of the individual as an employee, because of genetic information with respect to the individual (or information about a request for or the receipt of genetic services by such individual or family member of such individual); or (3) to cause or attempt to cause an employer to discriminate against an individual in violation of this title.	(a) Discrimination Based on Genetic Information.- It shall be an unlawful employment practice for an employment agency — (1) to fail or refuse to refer for employment, or otherwise to discriminate against, any individual because of genetic information with respect to the individual; (2) to limit, segregate, or classify individuals or fail or refuse to refer for employment any individual in any way that would deprive or tend to deprive any individual of employment opportunities, or otherwise adversely affect the status of the individual as an employee, because of genetic information with respect to the individual; or (3) to cause or attempt to cause an employer to discriminate against an individual in violation of this title.
Section 203(b)(1)	(b) Acquisition of Genetic Information- It shall be an unlawful employment practice for an employment agency to request, require, or purchase genetic information with respect to an individual or a family member of the individual (or information about a request for the receipt of genetic services by such individual or a family member of such individual) except — (1) where an employment agency inadvertently requests or requires family medical history of the individual or family member of the individual;	(b) Acquisition of Genetic Information- It shall be an unlawful employment practice for an employment agency to request, require, or purchase genetic information with respect to an individual or a family member of the individual except — (1) where an employment agency inadvertently requests or requires family medical history of the individual or family member of the individual;

Section 203(b)(2)	(2) where — (A) health or genetic services are offered by the employment agency, including such services offered as part of a bona fide wellness program; (B) the individual provides prior, knowing, voluntary, and written authorization; (C) only the individual (or family member if the family member is receiving genetic services) and the licensed health care professional or board certified genetic counselor involved in providing such services receive individually identifiable information concerning the results of such services; and (D) any individually identifiable genetic information provided under subparagraph (C) in connection with the services provided under subparagraph (A) is only available for purposes of such services and shall not be disclosed to the employment agency except in aggregate terms that do not disclose the identity of specific individuals;	Same as Senate subsection 203(b)(2).
Section 203(b)(3)-(4)	(3) where an employment agency requests or requires family medical history from the individual to comply with the certification provisions of section 103 of the Family and Medical Leave Act of 1993 (29 U.S.C. 2613) or such requirements under State family and medical leave laws; (4) where an employment agency purchases documents that are commercially and publicly available (including newspapers, magazines, periodicals, and books, but not including medical databases or court records) that include family medical history; or	Same as Senate subsections 203(b)(3)-(4).
Section 203(b)(5)(A)-(D)	(5) where the information involved is to be used for genetic monitoring of the biological effects of toxic substances in the workplace, but only if — (A) the employment agency provides written notice of the genetic monitoring to the individual; (B)(i) the individual provides prior, knowing, voluntary, and written authorization; or (ii) the genetic monitoring is required by Federal or State law; (C) the individual is informed of individual monitoring results; (D) the monitoring is in compliance with — (i) any Federal genetic monitoring regulations, including any such regulations that may be promulgated by the Secretary of Labor pursuant to the Occupational Safety and Health Act of 1970 (29 U.S.C. 651 et seq.), the Federal Mine Safety and Health Act of 1977 (30 U.S.C. 801 et seq.), or the Atomic Energy Act of 1954 (42 U.S.C. 2011 et seq.); or (ii) State genetic monitoring regulations, in the case of a State that is implementing genetic monitoring regulations under the authority of the Occupational Safety and Health Act of 1970 (29 U.S.C. 651 et seq.); and	Same as Senate subsection 203(b)(5)(A)-(D).

Table 1. (Continued).

	S. 358 (as reported by the HELP Committee, March 29, 2007)	H.R. 493 (as passed by the House, April 25, 2007)
Section 203(b)(5)(E)	(E) the employment agency, excluding any licensed health care professional or board certified genetic counselor that is involved in the genetic monitoring program, receives the results of the monitoring only in aggregate terms that do not disclose the identity of specific individuals;	Same as Senate subsection 203(b)(5)(E).
Section 203(c)	(c) Preservation of Protections- In the case of information to which any of paragraphs (1) through (5) of subsection (b) applies, such information may not be used in violation of paragraph (1) or (2) of subsection (a) or treated or disclosed in a manner that violates section 206.	(c) Preservation of Protections- In the case of information to which any of paragraphs (1) through (5) of subsection (b) applies, such information may not be used in violation of paragraph (1) , (2) or (3) of subsection (a) or treated or disclosed in a manner that violates section 206.
Section 204(a)	(a) Use of Genetic Information- It shall be an unlawful employment practice for a labor organization — (1) to exclude or to expel from the membership of the organization, or otherwise to discriminate against, any member because of genetic information with respect to the member (or information about a request for or the receipt of genetic services by such member or family member of such member); (2) to limit, segregate, or classify the members of the organization, or fail or refuse to refer for employment any member, in any way that would deprive or tend to deprive any member of employment opportunities, or otherwise adversely affect the status of the member as an employee, because of genetic information with respect to the member (or information about a request for or the receipt of genetic services by such member or family member of such member); or (3) to cause or attempt to cause an employer to discriminate against a member in violation of this title.	(a) Discrimination Based on Genetic Information. — It shall be an unlawful employment practice for a labor organization — (1) to exclude or to expel from the membership of the organization, or otherwise to discriminate against, any member because of genetic information with respect to the member; (2) to limit, segregate, or classify the members of the organization, or fail or refuse to refer for employment any member, in any way that would deprive or tend to deprive any member of employment opportunities, or otherwise adversely affect the status of the member as an employee, because of genetic information with respect to the member; or (3) to cause or attempt to cause an employer to discriminate against a member in violation of this title.
Section 204(b)(1)	(b) Acquisition of Genetic Information- It shall be an unlawful employment practice for a labor organization to request, require, or purchase genetic information with respect to a member or a family member of the member (or information about a request for the receipt of genetic services by such member or a family member of such member) except — (1) where a labor organization inadvertently requests or requires family medical history of the member or family member of the member;	(b) Acquisition of Genetic Information- It shall be an unlawful employment practice for a labor organization to request, require, or purchase genetic information with respect to a member or a family member of the member except — (1) where a labor organization inadvertently requests or requires family medical history of the member or family member of the member;

Section 204(b)(2)	(2) where — (A) health or genetic services are offered by the labor organization, including such services offered as part of a bona fide wellness program; (B) the member provides prior, knowing, voluntary, and written authorization; (C) only the member (or family member if the family member is receiving genetic services) and the licensed health care professional or board certified genetic counselor involved in providing such services receive individually identifiable information concerning the results of such services; and (D) any individually identifiable genetic information provided under subparagraph (C) in connection with the services provided under subparagraph (A) is only available for purposes of such services and shall not be disclosed to the labor organization except in aggregate terms that do not disclose the identity of specific members;	Same as Senate subsection 204(b)(2).
Section 204(b)(3)-(4)	(3) where a labor organization requests or requires family medical history from the members to comply with the certification provisions of section 103 of the Family and Medical Leave Act of 1993 (29 U.S.C. 2613) or such requirements under State family and medical leave laws; (4) where a labor organization purchases documents that are commercially and publicly available (including newspapers, magazines, periodicals, and books, but not including medical databases or court records) that include family medical history; or	Same as Senate subsections 204(b)(3)-(4).
Section 204(b)(5)(A)-(D)	(5) where the information involved is to be used for genetic monitoring of the biological effects of toxic substances in the workplace, but only if — (A) the labor organization provides written notice of the genetic monitoring to the member; (B)(i) the member provides prior, knowing, voluntary, and written authorization; or (ii) the genetic monitoring is required by Federal or State law; (C) the member is informed of individual monitoring results; (D) the monitoring is in compliance with — (i) any Federal genetic monitoring regulations, including any such regulations that may be promulgated by the Secretary of Labor pursuant to the Occupational Safety and Health Act of 1970 (29 U.S.C. 651 et seq.), the Federal Mine Safety and Health Act of 1977 (30 U.S.C. 801 et seq.), or the Atomic Energy Act of 1954 (42 U.S.C. 2011 et seq.); or (ii) State genetic monitoring regulations, in the case of a State that is implementing genetic monitoring regulations under the authority of the Occupational Safety and Health Act of 1970 (29 U.S.C. 651 et seq.); and	Same as Senate subsection 204(b)(5)(A)-(D).
Section 204(b)(5)(E)	(E) the labor organization, excluding any licensed health care professional or board certified genetic counselor that is involved in the genetic monitoring program, receives the results of the monitoring only in aggregate terms that do not disclose the identity of specific members;	Same as Senate subsection 204(b)(5)(E).

Table 1. (Continued).

	S. 358 (as reported by the HELP Committee, March 29, 2007)	H.R. 493 (as passed by the House, April 25, 2007)
Section 204(c)	(c) Preservation of Protections- In the case of information to which any of paragraphs (1) through (5) of subsection (b) applies, such information may not be used in violation of paragraph (1) or (2) of subsection (a) or treated or disclosed in a manner that violates section 206.	(c) Preservation of Protections- In the case of information to which any of paragraphs (1) through (5) of subsection (b) applies, such information may not be used in violation of paragraph (1), (2), or (3) of subsection (a) or treated or disclosed in a manner that violates section 206.
Section 205(a)	(a) Use of Genetic Information- It shall be an unlawful employment practice for any employer, labor organization, or joint labor-management committee controlling apprenticeship or other training or retraining, including on-the-job training programs — (1) to discriminate against any individual because of genetic information with respect to the individual (or information about a request for or the receipt of genetic services by such individual or a family member of such individual) in admission to, or employment in, any program established to provide apprenticeship or other training or retraining; (2) to limit, segregate, or classify the applicants for or participants in such apprenticeship or other training or retraining, or fail or refuse to refer for employment any individual, in any way that would deprive or tend to deprive any individual of employment opportunities, or otherwise adversely affect the status of the individual as an employee, because of genetic information with respect to the individual (or information about a request for or receipt of genetic services by such individual or family member of such individual); or (3) to cause or attempt to cause an employer to discriminate against an applicant for or a participant in such apprenticeship or other training or retraining in violation of this title.	(a) Discrimination Based on Genetic Information- It shall be an unlawful employment practice for any employer, labor organization, or joint labor-management committee controlling apprenticeship or other training or retraining, including on-the-job training programs — (1) to discriminate against any individual because of genetic information with respect to the individual in admission to, or employment in, any program established to provide apprenticeship or other training or retraining; (2) to limit, segregate, or classify the applicants for or participants in such apprenticeship or other training or retraining, or fail or refuse to refer for employment any individual, in any way that would deprive or tend to deprive any individual of employment opportunities, or otherwise adversely affect the status of the individual as an employee, because of genetic information with respect to the individual; or (3) to cause or attempt to cause an employer to discriminate against an applicant for or a participant in such apprenticeship or other training or retraining in violation of this title.

Section 205(b)(1)	(b) Acquisition of Genetic Information- It shall be an unlawful employment practice for an employer, labor organization, or joint labor-management committee described in subsection (a) to request, require, or purchase genetic information with respect to an individual or a family member of the individual (or information about a request for the receipt of genetic services by such individual or a family member of such individual) except — (1) where the employer, labor organization, or joint labor-management committee inadvertently requests or requires family medical history of the individual or family member of the individual;	(b) Acquisition of Genetic Information- It shall be an unlawful employment practice for an employer, labor organization, or joint labor-management committee described in subsection (a) to request, require, or purchase genetic information with respect to an individual or a family member of the individual except — (1) where the employer, labor organization, or joint labor-management committee inadvertently requests or requires family medical history of the individual or family member of the individual;
Section 205(b)(2)	(2) where — (A) health or genetic services are offered by the employer, labor organization, or joint labor-management committee, including such services offered as part of a bona fide wellness program; (B) the individual provides prior, knowing, voluntary, and written authorization; (C) only the individual (or family member if the family member is receiving genetic services) and the licensed health care professional or board certified genetic counselor involved in providing such services receive individually identifiable information concerning the results of such services; (D) any individually identifiable genetic information provided under subparagraph (C) in connection with the services provided under subparagraph (A) is only available for purposes of such services and shall not be disclosed to the employer, labor organization, or joint labor-management committee except in aggregate terms that do not disclose the identity of specific individuals;	Same as Senate subsection 205(b)(2).
Section 205(b)(3)-(4)	(3) where the employer, labor organization, or joint labor-management committee requests or requires family medical history from the individual to comply with the certification provisions of section 103 of the Family and Medical Leave Act of 1993 (29 U.S.C. 2613) or such requirements under State family and medical leave laws; (4) where the employer, labor organization, or joint labor-management committee purchases documents that are commercially and publicly available (including newspapers, magazines, periodicals, and books, but not including medical databases or court records) that include family medical history; or	Same as Senate subsections 205(b)(3)-(4).

Table 1. (Continued).

	S. 358 (as reported by the HELP Committee, March 29, 2007)	H.R. 493 (as passed by the House, April 25, 2007)
Section 205(b)(5)(A)-(D)	(5) where the information involved is to be used for genetic monitoring of the biological effects of toxic substances in the workplace, but only if — (A) the employer, labor organization, or joint labor-management committee provides written notice of the genetic monitoring to the individual; (B)(i) the individual provides prior, knowing, voluntary, and written authorization; or (ii) the genetic monitoring is required by Federal or State law; (C) the individual is informed of individual monitoring results; (D) the monitoring is in compliance with — (i) any Federal genetic monitoring regulations, including any such regulations that may be promulgated by the Secretary of Labor pursuant to the Occupational Safety and Health Act of 1970 (29 U.S.C. 651 et seq.), the Federal Mine Safety and Health Act of 1977 (30 U.S.C. 801 et seq.), or the Atomic Energy Act of 1954 (42 U.S.C. 2011 et seq.); or (ii) State genetic monitoring regulations, in the case of a State that is implementing genetic monitoring regulations under the authority of the Occupational Safety and Health Act of 1970 (29 U.S.C. 651 et seq.); and	Same as Senate subsections 205(b)(5)(A)-(D).
Section 205(b)(5)(E)	(E) the employer, labor organization, or joint labor-management committee, excluding any licensed health care professional or board certified genetic counselor that is involved in the genetic monitoring program, receives the results of the monitoring only in aggregate terms that do not disclose the identity of specific individuals;	Same as Senate subsection 205(b)(5)(E) except the word "or" is added at the end of the subsection.
Section 205(b)(6)	No comparable provision.	(6) where the employer conducts DNA analysis for law enforcement purposes as a forensic laboratory, includes such analysis in the Combined DNA Index System pursuant to section 210304 of the Violent Crime Control and Law Enforcement Act of 1994 (42 U.S.C. 14132), and requests or requires genetic information of such employer's apprentices or trainees, but only to the extent that such genetic information is used for analysis of DNA identification markers for quality control to detect sample contamination.

Section 205(c)	(c) Preservation of Protections- In the case of information to which any of paragraphs (1) through (5) of subsection (b) applies, such information may not be used in violation of paragraph (1) or (2) of subsection (a) or treated or disclosed in a manner that violates section 206.	(c) Preservation of Protections- In the case of information to which any of paragraphs (1) through (6) of subsection (b) applies, such information may not be used in violation of paragraph (1), (2), or (3) of subsection (a) or treated or disclosed in a manner that violates section 206.
Section 206(a)	(a) Treatment of Information as Part of Confidential Medical Record. — If an employer, employment agency, labor organization, or joint labor-management committee possesses genetic information about an employee or member (or information about a request for or receipt of genetic services by such employee or member or family member of such employee or member), such information shall be maintained on separate forms and in separate medical files and be treated as a confidential medical record of the employee or member.	(a) Treatment of Information as Part of Confidential Medical Record. — If an employer, employment agency, labor rganization, or joint labor-management committee possesses genetic information about an employee or member, such information shall be maintained on separate forms and in separate medical files and be treated as a confidential medical record of the employee or member. An employer, employment agency, labor organization, or joint labor-management committee shall be considered to be in compliance with the maintenance of information requirements of this subsection with respect to genetic information subject to this subsection that is maintained with and treated as a confidential medical record under section 102(d)(3)(B) of the Americans with Disabilities Act (42 U.S.C. 12112(d)(3)(B).

Table 1. (Continued).

	S. 358 (as reported by the HELP Committee, March 29, 2007)	H.R. 493 (as passed by the House, April 25, 2007)
Section 206(b)	Limitation on Disclosure. — An employer, employment agency, labor organization, or joint labor-management committee shall not disclose genetic information concerning an employee or member (or information about a request for or receipt of genetic services by such employee or member or family member of such employee or member) except — (1) to the employee (or family member if the family member is receiving the genetic services) or member of a labor organization at the request of the employee or member of such organization; (2) to an occupational or other health researcher if the research is conducted in compliance with the regulations and protections provided for under part 46 of title 45, Code of Federal Regulations; (3) in response to an order of a court, except that — (A) the employer, employment agency, labor organization, or joint labor-management committee may disclose only the genetic information expressly authorized by such order; and (B) if the court order was secured without the knowledge of the employee or member to whom the information refers, the employer, employment agency, labor organization, or joint labormanagement committee shall provide the employee or member with adequate notice to challenge the court order; (4) to government officials who are investigating compliance with this title if the information is relevant to the investigation; or (5) to the extent that such disclosure is made in connection with the employee's compliance with the certification provisions of section 103 of the Family and Medical Leave Act of 1993 (29 U.S.C. 2613) or such requirements under State family and medical leave laws.	Limitation on Disclosure. — An employer, employment agency, labor organization, or joint labor-management committee shall not disclose genetic information concerning an employee or member except — (1) to the employee or member of a labor organization (or family member if the family member is receiving the genetic services) at the written request of the employee or member of such organization; (2) to an occupational or other health researcher if the research is conducted in compliance with the regulations and protections provided for under part 46 of title 45, Code of Federal Regulations; (3) in response to an order of a court, except that — (A) the employer, employment agency, labor organization, or joint labor-management committee may disclose only the genetic information expressly authorized by such order; and (B) if the court order was secured without the knowledge of the employee or member to whom the information refers, the employer, employment agency, labor organization, or joint labor-management committee shall inform the employee or member of the court order and any genetic information that was disclosed pursuant to such order; (4) to government officials who are investigating compliance with this title if the information is relevant to the investigation; or (5) to the extent that such disclosure is made in connection with the employee's compliance with the certification provisions of section 103 of the Family and Medical Leave Act of 1993 (29 U.S.C. 2613) or such requirements under State family and medical leave laws.

Section 206(c)	No comparable provision	(c) Relationship to HIPAA Regulation. — With respect to the regulations promulgated by the Secretary of Health and Human Services under part C of title XI of the Social Security Act (42 U.S.C. 1320d et seq.) and section 264 of the Health Insurance Portability and Accountability Act of 1996 (42 U.S.C. 1320d-2 note), this title does not prohibit a covered entity under such regulations from any use or disclosure of health information that is authorized for the covered entity under such regulations. The previous sentence does not affect the authority of such Secretary to modify such regulations.
Section 207(a)(1)-(2)	(a) Employees Covered by Title VII of the Civil Rights Act of 1964- (1) IN GENERAL- The powers, remedies, and procedures provided in sections 705, 706, 707, 709, 710, and 711 of the Civil Rights Act of 1964 (42 U.S.C. 2000e-4 et seq.) to the Commission, the Attorney General, or any person, alleging a violation of title VII of that Act (42 U.S.C. 2000e et seq.) shall be the powers, remedies, and procedures this title provides to the Commission, the Attorney General, or any person, respectively, alleging an unlawful employment practice in violation of this title against an employee described in section 201(2)(A)(i), except as provided in paragraphs (2) and (3). (2) COSTS AND FEES- The powers, remedies, and procedures provided in subsections (b) and (c) of section 722 of the Revised Statutes (42 U.S.C. 1988), shall be powers, remedies, and procedures this title provides to the Commission, the Attorney General, or any person, alleging such a practice.	Subsections 207(a)(1)-(2) are the same in both bills except that where the Senate bill states "Revised Statutes," the House bill states "Revised Statutes of the United States."
Section 207(a)(3)	(3) DAMAGES- The powers, remedies, and procedures provided in section 1977A of the Revised Statutes (42 U.S.C. 1981a), including the limitations contained in subsection (b)(3) of such section 1977A, shall be powers, remedies, and procedures this title provides to the Commission, the Attorney General, or any person, alleging such a practice (not an employment practice specifically excluded from coverage under section 1977A(a)(1) of the Revised Statutes).	Section 207(a)(3) is the same in both bills except that where the Senate bill states "Revised Statutes," the House bill states "Revised Statutes of the United States."

Table 1. (Continued).

	S. 358 (as reported by the HELP Committee, March 29, 2007)	H.R. 493 (as passed by the House, April 25, 2007)
Section 207(b)(1)-(2)	(b) Employees Covered by Government Employee Rights Act of 1991- (1) IN GENERAL- The powers, remedies, and procedures provided in sections 302 and 304 of the Government Employee Rights Act of 1991 (42 U.S.C. 2000e-16b, 2000e-16c) to the Commission, or any person, alleging a violation of section 302(a)(1) of that Act (42 U.S.C. 2000e-16b(a)(1)) shall be the powers, remedies, and procedures this title provides to the Commission, or any person, respectively, alleging an unlawful employment practice in violation of this title against an employee described in section 201(2)(A)(ii), except as provided in paragraphs (2) and (3). (2) COSTS AND FEES- The powers, remedies, and procedures provided in subsections (b) and (c) of section 722 of the Revised Statutes (42 U.S.C. 1988), shall be powers, remedies, and procedures this title provides to the Commission, or any person, alleging such a practice.	Subsections 207(b)(1)-(2) are the same in both bills except that where the Senate bill states "Revised Statutes," the House bill states "Revised Statutes of the United States."
Section 207(b)(3)	(3) DAMAGES- The powers, remedies, and procedures provided in section 1977A of the Revised Statutes (42 U.S.C. 1981a), including the limitations contained in subsection (b)(3) of such section 1977A, shall be powers, remedies, and procedures this title provides to the Commission, or any person, alleging such a practice (not an employment practice specifically excluded from coverage under section 1977A(a)(1) of the Revised Statutes).	Subsection 207(b)(3) is the same in both bills except that where the Senate bill states "Revised Statutes," the House bill states "Revised Statutes of the United States."
Section 207(c)	(c) Employees Covered by Congressional Accountability Act of 1995- (1) IN GENERAL- The powers, remedies, and procedures provided in the Congressional Accountability Act of 1995 (2 U.S.C. 1301 et seq.) to the Board (as defined in section 101 of that Act (2 U.S.C. 1301)), or any person, alleging a violation of section 201(a)(1) of that Act (42 U.S.C. 1311(a)(1)) shall be the powers, remedies, and procedures this title provides to that Board, or any person, alleging an unlawful employment practice in violation of this title against an employee described in section 201(2)(A)(iii), except as provided in paragraphs (2) and (3). (2) COSTS AND FEES- The powers, remedies, and procedures provided in subsections (b) and (c) of section 722 of the Revised Statutes (42 U.S.C. 1988), shall be powers, remedies, and procedures this title provides to that Board, or any person, alleging such a practice. (3) DAMAGES- The powers, remedies, and procedures provided in section 1977A of the Revised Statutes (42 U.S.C. 1981a), including the limitations contained in subsection (b)(3) of such section 1977A, shall be powers, remedies, and procedures this title provides to that Board, or any person, alleging such a practice (not an employment practice specifically excluded from coverage under section 1977A(a)(1) of the Revised Statutes). (4) OTHER APPLICABLE PROVISIONS- With respect to a claim alleging a practice described in paragraph (1), title III of the Congressional Accountability Act of 1995 (2 U.S.C. 1381 et seq.) shall apply in the same manner as such title applies with respect to a claim alleging a violation of section 201(a)(1) of such Act (2 U.S.C. 1311(a)(1)).	Section 207(c) is the same in both bills except that where the Senate bill states "Revised Statutes," the House bill states "Revised Statutes of the United States."

Section 207(d)(1)-(2)	(d) Employees Covered by Chapter 5 of Title 3, United States Code- (1) IN GENERAL- The powers, remedies, and procedures provided in chapter 5 of title 3, United States Code, to the President, the Commission, the Merit Systems Protection Board, or any person, alleging a violation of section 411(a)(1) of that title, shall be the powers, remedies, and procedures this title provides to the President, the Commission, such Board, or any person, respectively, alleging an unlawful employment practice in violation of this title against an employee described in section 201(2)(A)(iv), except as provided in paragraphs (2) and (3). (2) COSTS AND FEES- The powers, remedies, and procedures provided in subsections (b) and (c) of section 722 of the Revised Statutes (42 U.S.C. 1988), shall be powers, remedies, and procedures this title provides to the President, the Commission, such Board, or any person, alleging such a practice.	Subsections 207(d)(1)-(2) are the same in both bills except that where the Senate bill states "Revised Statutes," the House bill states "Revised Statutes of the United States."
Section 207(d)(3)	(3) DAMAGES- The powers, remedies, and procedures provided in section 1977A of the Revised Statutes (42 U.S.C. 1981a), including the limitations contained in subsection (b)(3) of such section 1977A, shall be powers, remedies, and procedures this title provides to the President, the Commission, such Board, or any person, alleging such a practice (not an employment practice specifically excluded from coverage under section 1977A(a)(1) of the Revised Statutes).	Subsection 207(d)(3) is the same in both bills except that where the Senate bill states "Revised Statutes," the House bill states "Revised Statutes of the United States."
Section 207(e)(1)-(2)	(e) Employees Covered by Section 717 of the Civil Rights Act of 1964- (1) IN GENERAL- The powers, remedies, and procedures provided in section 717 of the Civil Rights Act of 1964 (42 U.S.C. 2000e-16) to the Commission, the Attorney General, the Librarian of Congress, or any person, alleging a violation of that section shall be the powers, remedies, and procedures this title provides to the Commission, the Attorney General, the Librarian of Congress, or any person, respectively, alleging an unlawful employment practice in violation of this title against an employee or applicant described in section 201(2)(A)(v), except as provided in paragraphs (2) and (3). (2) COSTS AND FEES- The powers, remedies, and procedures provided in subsections (b) and (c) of section 722 of the Revised Statutes (42 U.S.C. 1988), shall be powers, remedies, and procedures this title provides to the Commission, the Attorney General, the Librarian of Congress, or any person, alleging such a practice.	Subsections 207(e)(1)(2) are the same in both bills except that where the Senate bill states "Revised Statutes," the House bill states "Revised Statutes of the United States."
Section 207(e)(3)	(3) DAMAGES- The powers, remedies, and procedures provided in section 1977A of the Revised Statutes (42 U.S.C. 1981a), including the limitations contained in subsection (b)(3) of such section 1977A, shall be powers, remedies, and procedures this title provides to the Commission, the Attorney General, the Librarian of Congress, or any person, alleging such a practice (not an employment practice specifically excluded from coverage under section 1977A(a)(1) of the Revised Statutes).	Subsection 207(e)(3) is the same in both bills except that where the Senate bill states "Revised Statutes," the House bill states "Revised Statutes of the United States.

Table 1. (Continued).

	S. 358 (as reported by the HELP Committee, March 29, 2007)	H.R. 493 (as passed by the House, April 25, 2007)
Section 207(f)	(f) Definition- In this section, the term "Commission" means the Equal Employment Opportunity Commission.	Same as Senate subsection 207(f).
Section 208(a)-(b)	(a) General Rule- Notwithstanding any other provision of this Act, "disparate impact," as that term is used in section 703(k) of the ivil Rights Act of 1964 (42 U.S.C. 2000e-2(k)), on the basis of genetic information does not establish a cause of action under this Act. (b) Commission- On the date that is 6 years after the date of enactment of this Act, there shall be established a commission, to be known as the Genetic Nondiscrimination Study Commission (referred to in this section as the "Commission") to review the developing science of genetics and to make recommendations to Congress regarding whether to provide a disparate impact cause of action under this Act.	Same as Senate subsections 208(a)-(b).
Section 208(c)	(c) Membership- (1) IN GENERAL- The Commission shall be composed of 8 members, of which — (A) 1 member shall be appointed by the Majority Leader of the Senate; (B) 1 member shall be appointed by the Minority Leader of the Senate; (C) 1 member shall be appointed by the Chairman of the Committee on Health, Education, Labor, and Pensions of the Senate; (D) 1 member shall be appointed by the ranking minority member of the Committee on Health, Education, Labor, and Pensions of the Senate; (E) 1 member shall be appointed by the Speaker of the House of Representatives; (F) 1 member shall be appointed by the Minority Leader of the House of Representatives; (G) 1 member shall be appointed by the Chairman of the Committee on Education and the Workforce of the House of Representatives; and (H) 1 member shall be appointed by the ranking minority member of the Committee on Education and the Workforce of the House of Representatives. (2) COMPENSATION AND EXPENSES- The members of the Commission shall not receive compensation for the performance of services for the Commission, but shall be allowed travel expenses, including per diem in lieu of subsistence, at rates authorized for employees of agencies under subchapter I of chapter 57 of title 5, United States Code, while away from their homes or regular places of business in the performance of services for the Commission..	Same as Senate subsection 208(c).

Section 208(d)	(d) Administrative Provisions- (1) LOCATION- The Commission shall be located in a facility maintained by the Equal Employment Opportunity Commission. (2) DETAIL OF GOVERNMENT EMPLOYEES- Any Federa Government employee may be detailed to the Commission without reimbursement, and such detail shall be without interruption or loss of civil service status or privilege. (3) INFORMATION FROM FEDERAL AGENCIES- The Commission may secure directly from any Federal department or agency such information as the Commission considers necessary to carry out the provisions of this section. Upon request of the Commission, the head of such department or agency shall furnish such information to the Commission. (4) HEARINGS- The Commission may hold such hearings, sit and act at such times and places, take such testimony, and receive such evidence as the Commission considers advisable to carry out the objectives of this section, except that, to the extent possible, the Commission shall use existing data and research. (5) POSTAL SERVICES- The Commission may use the United States mails in the same manner and under the same conditions as other departments and agencies of the Federal Government.	Same as Senate subsection 208(d).
Section 208(e)-(f)	(e) Report- Not later than 1 year after all of the members are appointed to the Commission under subsection (c)(1), the Commission shall submit to Congress a report that summarizes the findings of the Commission and makes such recommendations for legislation as are consistent with this Act. (f) Authorization of Appropriations- There are authorized to be appropriated to the Equal Employment Opportunity Commission such sums as may be necessary to carry out this section.	Same as Senate subsections 208(e) and (f).

Table 1. (Continued).

	S. 358 (as reported by the HELP Committee, March 29, 2007)	H.R. 493 (as passed by the House, April 25, 2007)
Section 209	Nothing in this title shall be construed to — (1) limit the rights or protections of an individual under the Americans with Disabilities Act of 1990 (42 U.S.C. 12101 et seq.), including coverage afforded to individuals under section 102 of such Act (42 U.S.C. 12112), or under the Rehabilitation Act of 1973 (29 U.S.C. 701 et seq.); (2)(A) limit the rights or protections of an individual to bring an action under this title against an employer, employment agency, labor organization, or joint labor-management committee for a violation of this title; or (B) establish a violation under this title for an employer, employment agency, labor organization, or joint labormanagement committee of a provision of the amendments made by title I; (3) limit the rights or protections of an individual under any other Federal or State statute that provides equal or greater protection to an individual than the rights or protections provided for under this title; (4) apply to the Armed Forces Repository of Specimen Samples for the Identification of Remains; (5) limit or expand the protections, rights, or obligations of employees or employers under applicable workers' compensation laws; (6) limit the authority of a Federal department or agency to conduct or sponsor occupational or other health research that is conducted in compliance with the regulations contained in part 46 of title 45, Code of Federal Regulations (or any corresponding or similar regulations or rule); and (7) limit the statutory or regulatory authority of the Occupational Safety and Health Administration or the Mine Safety and Health Administration to promulgate or enforce workplace safety and health laws and regulations.	(a) In General. — Nothing in this title shall be construed to — (1) limit the rights or protections of an individual under any other Federal or State statute that provides equal or greater protection to an individual than the rights or protections provided for under this title, including the protections of an individual under the Americans with Disabilities Act of 1990 (42 U.S.C. 12101 et seq.), (including coverage afforded to individuals under section 102 of such Act (42 U.S.C. 12112)), or under the Rehabilitation Act of 1973 (29 U.S.C. 701 et seq.); (2)(A) limit the rights or protections of an individual to bring an action under this title against an employer, employment agency, labor organization, or joint labor-management committee for a violation of this title; or (B) provide for enforcement of, or penalties for violation of, any requirement or prohibition applicable to any employer, employment agency, labor organization, or joint labormanagement committee the enforcement of which, or penalties for which, are provided under the amendments made by title I; (3) apply to the Armed Forces Repository of Specimen Samples for the Identification of Remains; (4) limit or expand the protections, rights, or obligations of employees or employers under applicable workers' compensation laws; (5) limit the authority of a Federal department or agency to conduct or sponsor occupational or other health research that is conducted in compliance with the regulations contained in part 46 of title 45, Code of Federal Regulations (or any corresponding or

		similar regulations or rule); (6) limit the statutory or regulatory authority of the Occupational Safety and Health Administration or the Mine Safety and Health Administration to promulgate or enforce workplace safety and health laws and regulations; or (7) require any specific benefit for an employee or member or a family member of an employee or member under any group health plan or health insurance issuer offering group health insurance coverage in connection with a group health plan. (b) Genetic Information of a Fetus or Embryo. — Any reference in this title to genetic information concerning an individual or family member of an individual shall — (1) with respect to such an individual or family member of an individual who is a pregnant woman, include genetic information of any fetus carried by such pregnant woman; and (2) with respect to an individual or family member utilizing an assisted reproductive technology, include genetic information of any embryo legally held by the individual or family member.
Section 210	MEDICAL INFORMATION THAT IS NOT GENETIC INFORMATION. An employer, employment agency, labor organization, or joint labor-management committee shall not be considered to be in violation of this title based on the use, acquisition, or disclosure of medical information that is not genetic information about a manifested disease, disorder, or pathological condition of an employee or member, including a manifested disease, disorder, or pathological condition that has or may have a genetic basis.	Same as Senate subsection 210.
Section 211	REGULATIONS. Not later than 1 year after the date of enactment of this title, the Commission shall issue final regulations in an accessible format to carry out this title.	REGULATIONS. Not later than 1 year after the date of enactment of this title, the Commission shall issue final regulations to carry out this title.
Section 212	AUTHORIZATION OF APPROPRIATIONS. There are authorized to be appropriated such sums as may be necessary to carry out this title (except for section 208).	Same as Senate subsection 212.

Table 1. (Continued).

	S. 358 (as reported by the HELP Committee, March 29, 2007)	H.R. 493 (as passed by the House, April 25, 2007)
Section 213	EFFECTIVE DATE. This title takes effect on the date that is 18 months after the date of enactment of this Act.	Same as Senate section 213.
Section 301 (House)	No comparable provision.	GUARANTEE AGENCY COLLECTION RETENTION. Clause (ii) of section 428(c)(6)(A) of the Higher Education Act of 1965 (20 U.S.C. 1078(c)(6)(A)) is amended to read as follows: `(ii) an amount equal to 23 percent of such payments for use in accordance with section 422B, except that beginning October 1, 2007, and ending September 30, 2008, this subparagraph shall be applied by substituting "22 percent" for "23 percent...."
Section 301 (Senate) Section 302 (House)	SEVERABILITY. If any provision of this Act, an amendment made by this Act, or the application of such provision or amendment to any person or circumstance is held to be unconstitutional, the remainder of this Act, the amendments made by this Act, and the application of such provisions to any person or circumstance shall not be affected thereby.	Section 302 in the House bill is the same as Senate bill section 301.

REFERENCES

[1] All references to the House and Senate bills are to S. 358, as reported, and H.R. 493, as passed. The title I insurance provision of GINA is discussed in a companion report: CRS Report RL33988, *Genetic Nondiscrimination in Health Insurance: A Side-by-Side Comparison of the Title I Provision in H.R. 493 and S. 358*, by C. Stephen Redhead.

[2] Section 201(3), S. 358, as reported; Section 201(3), H.R. 493, as passed.

[3] Section 201(4), S. 358, as reported; Section 201(4), H.R. 493, as passed.

[4] Sections 202(a), 203(a), 204(a), and 205(a), S. 358, as reported.

[5] Sections 202(b)(6), 205(b)(6), H.R. 493, as passed.

[6] Section 206(a), H.R. 493, as passed.

[7] Section 206(c), H.R. 493, as passed.

[8] Section 209(b), H.R. 493, as passed.

In: Genetic Discrimination
Editor: Leana A. Albertson, pp. 87-94
ISBN: 978-1-60456-357-3

Chapter 5

GENETIC DISCRIMINATION IN HEALTH INSURANCE*

National Human Genome Research Institute

WHAT IS THE ISSUE?

More than a decade of research on the human genome has yielded a wealth of information. Scientists have mapped and sequenced the genome, identified individual genes or sets of genes that are associated with diseases ranging from Alzheimer's to diabetes and certain forms of cancer, and developed genetic tests to determine an individual's predisposition for some of these diseases. Developments and discoveries like these - and others likely to come in the years ahead - offer hope that many deadly illnesses can be diagnosed, treated and perhaps even cured both earlier and with better results than is now possible.

By learning more about their genetic makeup and susceptibility to certain diseases, people now have more choices, and potentially more control, when dealing with their health and future. Genetic information may lead people to ask their physicians to screen them regularly for certain diseases, to take preventive measures earlier in life, or even to rethink their reproductive plans and choices.

But genetic information can also be misused. It can be used to discriminate against people in health insurance and employment. People known to carry a gene that increases their likelihood of developing cancer, for example, may get turned down for health insurance. Without health insurance, it may be impossible for some people to get treatment for a disease that could be fatal. This may lead some people to decide against genetic testing for fear of what the results might show, and who might find out about them. It also could lead some people to decline participation in biomedical research such as studies of gene mutations associated with certain diseases that examine the history of families prone to those maladies.

Each of us probably has half a dozen or more genetic mutations that place us at risk for some disease. That does not mean that we will develop the disease, only that we are more likely to get it than people who do not have the same genetic mutations we do. As our knowledge of the human genome increases, more and more people will likely be identified as carriers of mutations associated with a greater risk of certain diseases. That means that virtually all people are potential victims of genetic discrimination in health insurance.

WHAT ARE THE PUBLIC CONCERNS?

As a result, Americans have become concerned about the possible misuse of genetic information, especially in health insurance and employment. A *Time* magazine/Cable News Network (CNN) poll, published in June 2000, found that 75 percent of those surveyed would not want their insurance company to have information about their genetic code. A 1998 survey released by the National Center for Genome Resources (NCGR) found that 85 percent of those polled think employers should not have access to information about their employees' genetic conditions, risks or predispositions.

People have reason to be concerned. Employer-sponsored health insurance plans in the private sector cover more than half of all Americans. Numerous reports in the news media and from expert groups have already uncovered instances where people were denied health insurance or coverage for particular conditions based on genetic information. In one case, a young boy, who had inherited an altered gene from his mother making him susceptible to a potentially fatal heart condition, was denied coverage by a health insurer when the boy's father lost his job and group coverage, and then tried to buy new insurance.

In 1993, the Ethical, Legal and Social Implications (ELSI) Working Group of the Human Genome Project issued a report titled "*Genetic Information and Health Insurance*". The report recommended that people be eligible for health insurance no matter what is known about their past, present or future health status. Two years later, the ELSI Working Group and the National Action Plan on Breast Cancer (NAPBC) jointly developed guidelines to assist federal and state agencies in preventing genetic discrimination in health insurance.

Further, the ELSI Working Group and NAPBC recommended that health insurers be prohibited from using genetic information or an individual's request for genetic services to deny or limit health insurance coverage, establish differential rates or have access to an individual's genetic information without that individual's written authorization. Written authorization, the groups said, should be required for each separate disclosure and should specify the recipient of the disclosed information.

Next, the National Human Genome Research Institute (NHGRI) and the United States Department of Energy, acting through the ELSI Working Group, cosponsored a series of workshops in the mid-1990s on genetic discrimination in health insurance and the workplace. The findings and recommendations of the workshop participants were published in *Science*: (*Genetic Information and the Workplace: Legislative Approaches and Policy Challenges* [sciencemag.org]) magazine, the monthly journal of the American Association for the Advancement of Science.

* source:http://www.genome.goc/10002328

WHAT ARE THE LEGISLATIVE PROTECTIONS?

Those recommendations, and earlier ones issued by the ELSI Working Group and NAPBC led, in part, to new legislation and policies at both the federal and state levels. The Health Insurance Portability and Accountability Act (HIPAA) of 1996 provided the first federal protections against genetic discrimination in health insurance. The act prohibited health insurers from excluding individuals from group coverage due to past or present medical problems, including genetic predisposition to certain diseases. It limited exclusions from group plans for preexisting conditions to 12 months and prohibited such exclusions for people who had been covered previously for that condition for 12 months or more. And the law specifically stated that genetic information in the absence of a current diagnosis of illness did not constitute a preexisting condition.

On the other hand, HIPAA did not prohibit health insurers from charging a higher rate to individuals based on their genetic makeup, prevent insurers from collecting genetic information or limit the disclosure of genetic information about individuals to insurers. Nor did it prevent insurers from requiring applicants to undergo genetic testing.

The next step in addressing the issue of genetic discrimination was taken by President Bill Clinton. The President had earlier supported proposed legislation that would have banned all health plans - group or individual - from denying coverage or raising premiums on the basis of genetic information. When the legislation failed to pass Congress, President Clinton issued an executive order (Executive Order 13145 to Prohibit Discrimination in Federal Employment Based on Genetic Information) in February 2000 prohibiting agencies of the federal government from obtaining genetic information about their employees or job applicants and from using genetic information in hiring and promotion decisions. In announcing the order, President Clinton said, "We must not allow advances in genetics to become the basis of discrimination against any individual or any group. We must never allow these discoveries to change the basic belief upon which our government, our society, and our system of ethics is founded - that all of us are created equal, entitled to equal treatment under the law."

Both before and since that Executive Order, a number of bills have been introduced into Congress to further deal with genetic discrimination in health insurance and employment. Nine bills were introduced in the 106th Congress (1999-2001) and four in the 107th Congress (2001-03). Meanwhile, 41 states have enacted legislation related to genetic discrimination in health insurance and 31 states have adopted laws regarding genetic discrimination in the workplace. The state laws regarding health insurance conform to HIPAA.

There continues to be a high degree of interest in these topics in state legislatures. More than one hundred bills were introduced in state legislatures in 2000 alone. Some would inaugurate protection from genetic discrimination while others would modify or clarify existing legislation.

Executive Order 13145 to Prohibit Discrimination in Federal Employment Based on Genetic Information February 8, 2000

By the authority vested in me as President of the United States by the Constitution and the laws of the United States of America, it is ordered as follows:

Section 1. Nondiscrimination in Federal Employment on the Basis of Protected Genetic Information

1-101. It is the policy of the Government of the United States to provide equal employment opportunity in Federal employment for all qualified persons and to prohibit discrimination against employees based on protected genetic information, or information about a request for or the receipt of genetic services. This policy of equal opportunity applies to every aspect of Federal employment.

1-102. The head of each Executive department and agency shall extend the policy set forth in section 1-101 to all its employees covered by section 717 of Title VII of the Civil Rights Act of 1964, as amended (42 U.S.C. 2000e-16).

1-103. Executive departments and agencies shall carry out the provisions of this order to the extent permitted by law and consistent with their statutory and regulatory authorities, and their enforcement mechanisms. The Equal Employment Opportunity Commission shall be responsible for coordinating the policy of the Government of the United States to prohibit discrimination against employees in Federal employment based on protected genetic information, or information about a request for or the receipt of genetic services.

Section 2. Requirements Applicable to Employing Departments and Agencies

1-201. Definitions

a. The term "employee" shall include an employee, applicant for employment, or former employee covered by section 717 of the Civil Rights Act of 1964, as amended (42 U.S.C. 2000e-16).
b. Genetic monitoring means the periodic examination of employees to evaluate acquired modifications to their genetic material, such as chromosomal damage or evidence of increased occurrence of mutations, that may have developed in the course of employment due to exposure to toxic substances in the workplace, in order to identify, evaluate, respond to the effects of, or control adverse environmental exposures in the workplace.
c. Genetic services means health services, including genetic tests, provided to obtain, assess, or interpret genetic information for diagnostic or therapeutic purposes, or for genetic education or counseling.
d. Genetic test means the analysis of human DNA, RNA, chromosomes, proteins, or certain metabolites in order to detect disease-related genotypes or mutations. Tests for metabolites fall within the definition of "genetic tests" when an excess or deficiency of the metabolites indicates the presence of a mutation or mutations. The conducting of metabolic tests by a department or agency that are not intended to reveal the presence of a mutation shall not be considered a violation of this order,

regardless of the results of the tests. Test results revealing a mutation shall, however, be subject to the provisions of this order.

e. Protected genetic information.

1. In general, protected genetic information means:

    a. information about an individual's genetic tests;
    b. information about the genetic tests of an individual's family members; or
    c. information about the occurrence of a disease, or medical condition or disorder in family members of the individual.

2. Information about an individual's current health status (including infor-mation about sex, age, physical exams, and chemical, blood, or urine analyses) is not protected genetic information unless it is described in subparagraph (1).

1-202

In discharging their responsibilities under this order, departments and agencies shall implement the following nondiscrimination requirements.

a. The employing department or agency shall not discharge, fail or refuse to hire, or otherwise discriminate against any employee with respect to the compensation, terms, conditions, or privileges of employment of that employee, because of protected genetic information with respect to the employee, or because of information about a request for or the receipt of genetic services by such employee.
b. The employing department or agency shall not limit, segregate, or classify employees in any way that would deprive or tend to deprive any employee of employment opportunities or otherwise adversely affect that employee's status, because of protected genetic information with respect to the employee or because of information about a request for or the receipt of genetic services by such employee.
c. The employing department or agency shall not request, require, collect, or purchase protected genetic information with respect to an employee, or information about a request for or the receipt of genetic services by such employee.
d. The employing department or agency shall not disclose protected genetic information with respect to an employee, or information about a request for or the receipt of genetic services by an employee except:

    1. to the employee who is the subject of the information, at his or her request;
    2. to an occupational or other health researcher, if the research conducted complies with the regulations and protections provided for under part 46 of title 45, of the Code of Federal Regulations;
    3. if required by a Federal statute, congressional subpoena, or an order issued by a court of competent jurisdiction, except that if the subpoena or court order was secured without the knowledge of the individual to whom the information refers, the employer shall provide the individual with adequate notice to challenge the subpoena or court order, unless the subpoena or court order also imposes confidentiality requirements; or

4. to executive branch officials investigating compliance with this order, if the information is relevant to the investigation. the receipt of genetic services in general personnel files; such information shall be treated as confidential medical records and kept separate from personnel files.

Section 3. Exceptions

1-301

The following exceptions shall apply to the nondiscrimination requirements set forth in section 1-202.

a. The employing department or agency may request or require information defined in section 1-201(e)(1)(C) with respect to an applicant who has been given a conditional offer of employment or to an employee if:

   1. the request or requirement is consistent with the Rehabilitation Act and other applicable law;
   2. the information obtained is to be used exclusively to assess whether further medical evaluation is needed to diagnose a current disease, or medical condition or disorder, or under the terms of section 1-301(b) of this order;
   3. such current disease, or medical condition or disorder could prevent the applicant or employee from performing the essential functions of the position held or desired; and
   4. the information defined in section 1-201(e)(1)(C) of this order will not be disclosed to persons other than medical personnel involved in or responsible for assessing whether further medical evaluation is needed to diagnose a current disease, or medical condition or disorder, or under the terms of section 1-301(b) of this order.

b. The employing department or agency may request, collect or purchase protected genetic information with respect to an employee, or any information about a request for or receipt of genetic services by such employee if:

   1. the employee uses genetic or health care services provided by the employer (other than use pursuant to section 1-301(a) of this order);
   2. the employee who uses the genetic or health care services has provided prior knowing, voluntary, and written authorization to the employer to collect protected genetic information;
   3. the person who performs the genetic or health care services does not disclose protected genetic information to anyone except to the employee who uses the services for treatment of the individual; pursuant to section 1-202(d) of this order; for program evaluation or assessment; for compiling and analyzing information in anticipation of or for use in a civil or criminal legal proceeding; or, for payment or accounting purposes, to verify that the service was performed (but in such cases the genetic information itself cannot be disclosed);

4. such information is not used in violation of sections 1-202(a) or 1-202(b) of this order.

c. The employing department or agency may collect protected genetic information with respect to an employee if the requirements of part 46 of title 45 of the Code of Federal Regulations are met.
d. Genetic monitoring of biological effects of toxic substances in the workplace shall be permitted if all of the following conditions are met:

1. the employee has provided prior, knowing, voluntary and written authorization;
2. the employee is notified when the results of the monitoring are available and, at that time, the employer makes any protected genetic information that may have been acquired during the monitoring available to the employee and informs the employee how to obtain such information;
3. the monitoring conforms to any genetic monitoring regulations that may be promulgated by the Secretary of Labor; and ults of the monitoring only in aggregate terms that do not disclose the identity of specific employees.

e. This order does not limit the statutory authority of a Federal department or agency to:

1. promulgate or enforce workplace safety and health laws and regulations;
2. conduct or sponsor occupational or other health research that is conducted in compliance with regulations at part 46 of title 45, of the Code of Federal Regulations; or
3. collect protected genetic information as a part of a lawful program, the primary purpose of which is to carry out identification purposes.

Section 4. Miscellaneous

1-401

The head of each department and agency shall take appropriate action to disseminate this policy and, to this end, shall designate a high level official responsible for carrying out its responsibilities under this order.

1-402

Nothing in this order shall be construed to:

a. limit the rights or protections of an individual under the Rehabilitation Act of 1973 (29 U.S.C. 701, et seq.), the Privacy Act of 1974 (5 U.S.C. 552a), or other applicable law; or
b. require specific benefits for an employee or dependent under the Federal Employees Health Benefits Program or similar program.

1-403

This order clarifies and makes uniform Administration policy and does not create any right or benefit, substantive or procedural, enforceable at law by a party against the United States, its officers or employees, or any other person.

THE WHITE HOUSE
February 8, 2000.

In: Genetic Discrimination
Editor: Leana J. Albertson, pp. 95-106
ISBN: 978-1-60456-357-3

Chapter 6

GENETIC NONDISCRIMINATION IN HEALTH INSURANCE: A SIDE-BY-SIDE COMPARISON OF THE TITLE I PROVISIONS IN H.R. 493 AND S. 358*

C. Stephen Redhead

ABSTRACT

On April 25, the House passed the Genetic Information Nondiscrimination Act of 2007, H.R. 493, on a vote of 420-3. The Senate Health, Education, Labor, and Pensions (HELP) Committee approved similar legislation (S. 358). S. 358 is awaiting Senate floor action. The Genetic Information Nondiscrimination Act would restrict health insurers' (Title I) and employers' (Title II) acquisition and use of genetic information in several ways. These restrictions build upon those already imposed in federal law.

This report provides a comparison of the Title I provisions in H.R. 493 and S. 358. Those provisions would extend the current Health Insurance Portability and Accountability Act (HIPAA) protections against discrimination by group health plans and issuers of health insurance in both the group and individual markets, and restrict their collection, use and disclosure of genetic information.

INTRODUCTION

On April 25, the House passed the Genetic Information Nondiscrimination Act of 2007, H.R. 493, on a vote of 420-3. Earlier, the measure was reported by the Education and Labor Committee (H.Rept. 110-28, Part I), the Ways and Means Committee (H.Rept. 110-28, Part II), and the Energy and Commerce Committee (H.Rept. 110-28, Parts III and IV). The Senate Health, Education, Labor, and Pensions (HELP) Committee approved similar legislation (S. 358) on March 29, and filed its report (S.Rept. 110-48) on April 10. S. 358 is awaiting Senate floor action. The Genetic Information Nondiscrimination Act would restrict health insurers'

* Excerpted from CRS Report RL33988, dated May 2, 2007.

and employers' acquisition and use of genetic information in several ways. These restrictions build upon those already imposed in federal law.

OVERVIEW OF TITLE I PROVISIONS IN H.R. 493 AND S. 358

Title 1 of H.R. 493 / S. 358 would extend the current Health Insurance Portability and Accountability Act (HIPAA) protections against discrimination by group health plans and issuers of health insurance in both the group and individual markets, and restrict their acquisition, use and disclosure of genetic information. The HIPAA nondiscrimination provisions appear in three separate statutes: (1) the Employee Retirement Income Security Act (ERISA, Part 7), which regulates employee benefit plans, including employer-sponsored group health plans; (2) the Internal Revenue Code (IRC, Chapter 100), which also covers group health plans (using a slightly broader definition than ERISA); and (3) the Public Health Service Act (PHSA, Title XVII), which applies to insurance companies and managed care organizations, and to non-federal government health plans. H.R. 493, but not S. 358, would amend the HIPAA nondiscrimination provisions in all three statutes, as well as amending comparable provisions in the Medicare statute (Social Security Act Title XVIII) relating to supplementary health insurance benefits (Medigap).

Table 1, beginning on page 3, provides a side-by-side comparison of the two bills, using the House-passed measure as the referent. The table only includes the provisions in Title I (Genetic Nondiscrimination in Health Insurance). A separate CRS Report, RL33987, *Genetic Non-discrimination in Employment: A Comparison of Title II Provisions in S. 358 and H.R. 493, 110th Congress*, by Nancy Lee Jones, discusses the Title II employment provisions.

While the Title I provisions in the two bills are broadly similar there are a number of significant differences, including the following.

- Whereas H.R. 493 would amend the four federal statutes (i.e., ERISA, IRC, PHSA, and Medigap), S. 358 would amend only three; it does not include any provisions to amend IRC.
- H.R. 493, but not S. 358, includes a provision relating to the genetic information of a fetus or embryo. It provides that references to genetic information include genetic information on a fetus carried by a pregnant woman and, with respect to an individual utilizing assisted reproductive technology, includes genetic information of any embryo legally held by the individual or family member.
- In H.R. 493, language that prohibits the collection of genetic information by health plans and insurers for the purposes of underwriting and related activities appears in each of the four sections amending federal law. Comparable language in S. 358 appears only once in the privacy section (Sec. 104).
- Whereas both bills include provisions that would allow the relevant Secretary (Labor, Treasury, HHS) to impose the same monetary penalties for violations of the Title's nondiscrimination provisions, S. 358 includes additional remedies and enforcement provisions in its amendments to ERISA.

Table 1. Genetic Nondiscrimination in Health Insurance: H.R. 493 (Title I) vs. S. 358 (Title I)

H.R. 493 (as passed by the House, April 25, 2007)	S. 358 (as reported by the HELP Committee, March 29, 2007)
Amendments to ERISA Part 7 (Group Market Requirements) — Section 101	
No provision.	Clarifies that the ERISA provision prohibiting group health plans and insurance issuers from denying an individual eligibility to enroll in a group based on that individual's genetic information includes information about a request for or receipt of genetic services by that individual or a family member.
Prohibits group health plans and insurance issuers from adjusting a group's premium on the basis of genetic information.	Prohibits group health plans and insurance issuers from adjusting a group's premium based on an individual's (or family member's) genetic information, including information about a request for or receipt of genetic services by that individual or a family member.
Prohibits group health plans and insurance issuers from requesting or requiring that an individual or a family member of such individual undergo a genetic test. Does not limit the authority of a health care professional who is providing health care to an individual to request that the individual undergo a genetic test. Does not preclude a group health plan or insurance issuer from obtaining and using genetic test information for payment determinations (only the minimum amount of information necessary to accomplish the intended purpose may be requested). Permits a group health plan or insurance issuer to request, but not require, that an individual voluntarily undergo a genetic test as part of a research project.	.Prohibits group health plans and insurance issuers from requesting or requiring that an individual or a family member of such individual undergo a genetic test. Does not limit the authority of a health care professional who is providing health care to an individual to request that the individual (or a family member) undergo a genetic test. Does not limit the authority of a health care professional employed by or affiliated with a group health plan or insurance issuer, and who is providing health care services to an individual as part of a wellness program, to notify such individual about the availability of a genetic test. Does not permit a health care professional to require that an individual undergo a genetic test.
Prohibits group health plans and insurance insurers from requesting, requiring, or purchasing genetic information for the purposes of underwriting, eligibility determination (before or during the enrollment process), premium rating, or other activities related to the creation, renewal, or replacement of a health insurance plan or contract. Obtaining genetic information incidental to the acquisition of other information would not be considered a violation.	[Note: comparable language prohibiting the collection of genetic information is in Section 104 (Privacy and Confidentiality) of S. 358; see below.]
Applies the above nondiscrimination provisions to all group health plans. Clarifies that any reference to genetic information about an individual or family member who is pregnant shall include genetic information about the fetus. Clarifies that any reference to genetic information about an individual or family member using assisted reproductive technology shall include genetic information about any fetus legally held by that individual or family member.	Applies the above nondiscrimination provisions to all group health plans. No provisions.
Defines *family member* to include an individual's dependent through marriage, birth, or adoption or placement for adoption, as well as any first-, second-, third-, or fourth-degree relative of the individual or dependent.	Defines *family member* to include an individual's spouse and dependent children (including those born to or placed for adoption with the individual), as well as all others related by blood to the individual, the spouse, or the dependent or adopted children.

Defines *genetic information* as information about an individual's genetic tests, or those of family members, as well as information about family members' manifest diseases or disorders, to the extent that such information is taken into account as genetic information about other individuals. The term genetic information also includes any request for, or receipt of, genetic services (defined below) by an individual or family member. Does not include age and sex of individual.	Defines *genetic information* as information about an individual's genetic tests, or those of family members, as well as information about the occurrence of a disease or disorder in family members. Does not include age and sex of individual.
Defines *genetic test* as an analysis of DNA, RNA, chromosomes, proteins, or metabolites that detects genotypes, mutations, or chromosomal changes. Genetic test does not include an analysis of proteins or metabolites that is directly related to a manifest disease, disorder or pathological condition.	Same provisions.
Defines *genetic services* as a genetic test, genetic counseling, or genetic education.	Same provisions.
Authorizes the Labor Secretary to impose monetary penalties, subject to certain conditions, for violation of the above nondiscrimination provisions. [Note: these penalties are the same as the tax penalties in Section 4980D of the IRC.]	Same provisions.
No provisions.	Provides for injunctive relief prior to the exhaustion of available administrative remedies if the preponderance of evidence shows that the exhaustion of such remedies would cause irreparable harm to the health of the participant or beneficiary.
No provisions.	Provides for administrative penalties of $100 per day and the retroactive reinstatement of coverage for violations of the above nondiscrimination provisions.
Requires the Labor Secretary to issue final implementing regulations within one year. Amendments apply to plan years beginning after 18 months from enactment.	Same provisions.
Amendments to the Public Health Service Act Title XVII (Group Market Requirements) — Section 102(a)	
No provision.	Clarifies that the PHS Act provision prohibiting group health plans and insurance issuers from denying an individual eligibility to enroll in a group based on that individual's genetic information includes information about a request for or receipt of genetic services by that individual or a family member.
Prohibits group health plans and insurance issuers from adjusting a group's premium on the basis of genetic information.	Prohibits group health plans and insurance issuers from adjusting a group's premium based on an individual's (or family member's) genetic information, including information about a request for or receipt of genetic services by that individual or a family member.

Table 1. (Continued).

H.R. 493 (as passed by the House, April 25, 2007)	S. 358 (as reported by the HELP Committee, March 29, 2007)
Prohibits group health plans and insurance issuers from requesting or requiring that an individual or a family member of such individual undergo a genetic test. Does not limit the authority of a health care professional who is providing health care to an individual to request that the individual undergo a genetic test. Does not preclude a group health plan or insurance issuer from obtaining and using genetic test information for payment determinations (only the minimum amount of information necessary to accomplish the intended purpose may be requested). Permits a group health plan or insurance issuer to request, but not require, that an individual voluntarily undergo a genetic test as part of a research project.	Prohibits group health plans and insurance issuers from requesting or requiring that an individual or a family member of such individual undergo a genetic test. Does not limit the authority of a health care professional who is providing health care to an individual to request that the individual (or a family member) undergo a genetic test. Does not limit the authority of a health care professional employed by or affiliated with a group health plan or insurance issuer, and who is providing health care services to an individual as part of a wellness program, to notify such individual about the availability of a genetic test. Does not permit a health care professional to require that an individual undergo a genetic test.
Prohibits group health plans and insurance issuers from requesting, requiring, or purchasing genetic information for the purposes of underwriting, eligibility determination (before or during the enrollment process), premium rating, or other activities related to the creation, renewal, or replacement of a health insurance plan or contract. Obtaining genetic information incidental to the acquisition of other information would not be considered a violation.	[Note: comparable language prohibiting the collection of genetic information is in Section 104 (Privacy and Confidentiality) of S. 358; see below.]
Applies the above nondiscrimination provisions to all group health plans.	Applies the above nondiscrimination provisions to all group health plans.
Clarifies that any reference to genetic information about an individual or family member who is pregnant shall include genetic information about the fetus. Clarifies that any reference to genetic information about an individual or family member using assisted reproductive technology shall include genetic information about any fetus legally held by that individual or family member.	No provisions.
Defines *family member* to include an individual's dependent through marriage, birth, or adoption or placement for adoption, as well as any first-, second-, third-, or fourth-degree relative of the individual or dependent.	Defines *family member* to include an individual's spouse and dependent children (including those born to or placed for adoption with the individual), as well as all others related by blood to the individual, the spouse, or the dependent or adopted children.
Defines *genetic information* as information about an individual's genetic tests, or those of family members, as well as information about family members' manifest diseases or disorders, to the extent that such information is taken into account as genetic information about other individuals. The term genetic information also includes any request for, or receipt of, genetic services (defined below) by an individual or family member. Does not include age and sex of individual.	Defines *genetic information* as information about an individual's genetic tests, or those of family members, as well as information about the occurrence of a disease or disorder in family members. Does not include age and sex of individual.
Defines *genetic test* as an analysis of DNA, RNA, chromosomes, proteins, or metabolites that detects genotypes, mutations, or chromosomal changes. Genetic test does not include an analysis of proteins or metabolites that is directly related to a manifest disease, disorder or pathological condition.	Same provisions.

Defines *genetic services* as a genetic test, genetic counseling, or genetic education.	Same provisions.
Authorizes the HHS Secretary to impose monetary penalties, subject to certain conditions, for violation of the above nondiscrimination provisions. Note: these penalties are the same as the tax penalties in Section 4980D of the IRC.	Same provisions.
Requires the HHS Secretary to issue final implementing regulations within one year. Amendments apply to plan years beginning after 18 months from enactment.	Same provisions.
Amendments to the Public Health Service Act Title XVII (Individual Market Requirements) — Section 102(b)	
Prohibits insurance issuers from denying eligibility, adjusting premiums, or imposing any preexisting condition exclusion on the basis of genetic information.	Prohibits insurance issuers from denying eligibility or adjusting premiums based on an individual's (or family member's) genetic information, including information about a request for or receipt of genetic services by that individual or a family member.
Prohibits insurance issuers from requesting or requiring that an individual or a family member of such individual undergo a genetic test. Does not limit the authority of a health care professional who is providing health care to an individual to request that the individual undergo a genetic test. Does not preclude a group health plan or insurance issuer from obtaining and using genetic test information for payment determinations (only the minimum amount of information necessary to accomplish the intended purpose may be requested). Permits a group health plan or insurance issuer to request, but not require, that an individual voluntarily undergo a genetic test as part of a research project.	Prohibits insurance issuers from requesting or requiring that an individual or a family member of such individual undergo a genetic test. Does not limit the authority of a health care professional who is providing health care to an individual to request that the individual (or a family member) undergo a genetic test. Does not limit the authority of a health care professional employed by or affiliated with a health plan or insurance issuer, and who is providing health care services to an individual as part of a wellness program, to notify such individual about the availability of a genetic test. Does not permit a health care professional to require that an individual undergo a genetic test.
Prohibits insurance issuers from requesting, requiring, or purchasing genetic information for the purposes of underwriting, eligibility determination (before or during the enrollment process), premium rating, or other activities related to the creation, renewal, or replacement of a health insurance plan or contract. Obtaining genetic information incidental to the acquisition of other information would not be considered a violation.	[Note: comparable language prohibiting the collection of genetic information is in Section 104 (Privacy and Confidentiality) of S. 358; see below.]
Clarifies that any reference to genetic information about an individual or family member who is pregnant shall include genetic information about the fetus. Clarifies that any reference to genetic information about an individual or family member using assisted reproductive technology shall include genetic information about any fetus legally held by that individual or family member.	No provisions.
For violations of the above nondiscrimination provisions, grants the HHS Secretary the same enforcement authority with respect to insurance issuers in the individual market as the Secretary has for violations by insurance issuers in the small group market.	Same provisions.
Eliminates the option of non-federal government plans to be excepted from the above genetic nondiscrimination provisions.	Same provision.
Requires the HHS Secretary to issue final implementing regulations within one year. Amendments apply to insurance coverage offered, sold, issued, renewed, or in effect beginning 18 months after enactment.	Same provisions.

Table 1. (Continued).

H.R. 493 (as passed by the House, April 25, 2007)	S. 358 (as reported by the HELP Committee, March 29, 2007)
Amendments to the Internal Revenue Code Chapter 100 (Group Health Plan Requirements) — Section 103	
Prohibits group health plans from adjusting a group's premium on the basis of genetic information.	No provision.
Prohibits group health plans from requesting or requiring that an individual or a family member of such individual undergo a genetic test. Does not limit the authority of a health care professional who is providing health care to an individual to request that the individual undergo a genetic test. Does not preclude a group health plan from obtaining and using genetic test information for payment determinations (only the minimum amount of information necessary to accomplish the intended purpose may be requested). Permits a group health plan to request, but not require, that an individual voluntarily undergo a genetic test as part of a research project.	No provisions.
Prohibits group health plans from requesting, requiring, or purchasing genetic information for the purposes of underwriting, eligibility determination (before or during the enrollment process), premium rating, or other activities related to the creation, renewal, or replacement of a health insurance plan or contract. Obtaining genetic information incidental to the acquisition of other information would not be considered a violation.	No provisions.
Applies the above nondiscrimination provisions to all group health plans.	No provision.
Clarifies that any reference to genetic information about an individual or family member who is pregnant shall include genetic information about the fetus. Clarifies that any reference to genetic information about an individual or family member using assisted reproductive technology shall include genetic information about any fetus legally held by that individual or family member.	No provisions.
Defines *family member* to include an individual's dependent through marriage, birth, or adoption or placement for adoption, as well as any first-, second-, third-, or fourth-degree relative of the individual or dependent.	No provisions.
Defines *genetic information* as information about an individual's genetic tests, or those of family members, as well as information about family members' manifest diseases or disorders, to the extent that such information is taken into account as genetic information about other individuals. The term genetic information also includes any request for, or receipt of, genetic services (defined below) by an individual or family member. Does not include age and sex of individual.	No provisions.

Defines *genetic test* as an analysis of DNA, RNA, chromosomes, proteins, or metabolites that detects genotypes, mutations, or chromosomal changes. Genetic test does not include an analysis of proteins or metabolites that is directly related to a manifest disease, disorder or pathological condition.	No provisions.
Defines *genetic services* as a genetic test, genetic counseling, or genetic education.	No provisions.
Clarifies that group health plans that fail to meet the requirements set out in Chapter 100 of the IRC, which include the above nondiscrimination provisions, will be subject to the tax penalties in Section 4980D of the IRC.	No provisions.
Requires the Treasury Secretary to issue final implementing regulations within one year. Amendments apply to plan years beginning at least 18 months after enactment.	No provisions.
Amendments to Social Security Act Title XVIII (Medicare) Relating to Medigap — Section 104 (H.R. 493), Section 103 (S. 358)	
Prohibits an issuer of a Medigap policy from: (1) denying or conditioning the issuance or effectiveness of a policy; or (2) discriminating in the pricing of a policy, on the basis of genetic information.	Prohibits an issuer of a Medigap policy from: (1) denying or conditioning the issuance or effectiveness of a policy, or (2) discriminating in the pricing of a policy, based on an individual's (or family member's) genetic information, including information about a request for or receipt of genetic services by that individual or a family member.
Prohibits an issuer of a Medigap policy from requesting or requiring that an individual or a family member of such individual undergo a genetic test. Does not limit the authority of a health care professional who is providing health care to an individual to request that the individual undergo a genetic test. Does not preclude an issuer of a Medigap policy from obtaining and using genetic test information for payment determinations (only the minimum amount of information necessary to accomplish the intended purpose may be requested). Permits an issuer of a Medigap policy to request, but not require, that an individual voluntarily undergo a genetic test as part of a research project.	Prohibits an issuer of a Medigap policy from requesting or requiring that an individual or a family member undergo a genetic test. Does not limit the authority of a health care professional who is providing health care to an individual to request that the individual (or a family member) undergo a genetic test. Does not limit the authority of a health care professional employed by or affiliated with a health plan or insurance issuer, and who is providing health care services to an individual as part of a wellness program, to notify such individual about the availability of a genetic test. Does not permit a health care professional to require that an individual undergo a genetic test.
Prohibits an issuer of a Medigap policy from requesting, requiring, or purchasing genetic information for the purposes of underwriting, eligibility determination (before or during the enrollment process), premium rating, or other activities related to the creation, renewal, or replacement of a health insurance plan or contract. Obtaining genetic information incidental to the acquisition of other information would not be considered a violation.	[Note: comparable language prohibiting the collection of genetic information is in Section 104 (Privacy and Confidentiality) of S. 358; see below.]
Defines *family member* to include any first-, second-, third-, or fourth-degree relative of the individual.	Defines *family member* to include an individual's spouse and dependent children (including those born to or placed for adoption with the individual), as well as all others related by blood to the individual, the spouse, or the dependent or adopted children.

Table 1. (Continued).

H.R. 493 (as passed by the House, April 25, 2007)	S. 358 (as reported by the HELP Committee, March 29, 2007)
Defines *genetic information* as information about an individual's genetic tests, or those of family members, as well as information about family members' manifest diseases or disorders. The term genetic information also includes any request for, or receipt of, genetic services (defined below) by an individual or family member. Does not include age and sex of individual.	Defines *genetic information* as information about an individual's genetic tests, or those of family members, as well as information about the occurrence of a disease or disorder in family members. Does not include age and sex of individual.
Defines *genetic test* as an analysis of DNA, RNA, chromosomes, proteins, or metabolites that detects genotypes, mutations, or chromosomal changes. Genetic test does not include an analysis of proteins or metabolites that is directly related to a manifest disease, disorder or pathological condition.	Same provisions.
Defines *genetic services* as a genetic test, genetic counseling, or genetic education.	Same provisions.
Defines issuer of a Medigap policy to include a third-party administrator or other person acting for or on behalf of such issuer.	Same provisions.
Clarifies that any reference to genetic information about an individual or family member who is pregnant shall include genetic information about the fetus. Clarifies that any reference to genetic information about an individual or family member using assisted reproductive technology shall include genetic information about any fetus legally held by that individual or family member.	No provisions.
Applies to Medigap policies beginning at least 18 months after enactment.	Applies to Medigap policies beginning at least 18 months after enactment.
A state identified by the HHS Secretary as requiring a change in its statutes or regulations to conform its regulatory program to the requirements of this section would have until October 1, 2008, to make such a change before being considered out of compliance. States requiring a statutory change that do not meet in legislative session in 2008 would be given additional time to come into compliance. The bill would give the National Association of Insurance Commissioners (NAIC) until June 30, 2008, to modify its model regulation to conform to the requirements of this section. If NAIC failed to meet that deadline, the HHS Secretary would have until October 1, 2008, to make the modifications.	Same provisions.

Privacy and Confidentiality — Section 105 (H.R. 493), Section 104 (S. 358)	
Amends HIPAA to require the HHS Secretary, by rulemaking, to revise the HIPAA privacy rule as follows: (1) genetic information (as defined in the bill) would be treated as health information under the privacy rule; and (2) the use and disclosure of genetic information by a group health plan, health insurance issuer, or issuer of a Medigap policy for underwriting and other activities related to the creation, renewal, or replacement of a contract of health insurance or health benefits would be prohibited. Requires the HHS Secretary to publish the revisions as a notice in the *Federal Register*, not later than 60 days after enactment. The revisions would take effect upon publication without any prior public comment, but may be further modified, after opportunity for public comment.	Applies the HIPAA privacy rule protections to the use and disclosure of genetic information (as defined in this act). Prohibits a group health plan, health insurance issuer, or issuer of a Medigap policy from using or disclosing genetic information (including information about a request for or receipt of genetic services by an individual or family member) for underwriting, premium rating, or other activities related to the creation, renewal, or replacement of a contract of health insurance or health benefits.
[Note: similar language prohibiting the collection of genetic information appears in each of Sections 101 — 104; see above.]	Prohibits a group health plan, health insurance issuer, or issuer of a Medigap policy from requesting, requiring, or purchasing genetic information (including information about a request for or receipt of genetic services by an individual or family member) for underwriting, eligibility determination (before or during the enrollment process), premium rating, or other activities related to the creation, renewal, or replacement of a contract for health insurance or health benefits. Obtaining genetic information incidental to the acquisition of other information would not be considered a violation.
No comparable provisions.	The above privacy and confidentiality provisions would not apply to plans, insurers, and Medigap issuers that are not HIPAA covered entities, nor would they apply to genetic information that is not considered individually identifiable under the HIPAA privacy rule.
Provides that any group health plan, health insurance issuer, or issuer of a Medigap policy who violates the privacy rule with respect to the use or disclosure of genetic information would be subject to the civil and criminal penalties set out in the Administrative Simplification provisions of HIPAA.	Provides that any group health plan, health insurance issuer, or issuer of a Medigap policy who violates the above privacy and confidentiality provisions would be subject to the civil and criminal penalties set out in the Administrative Simplification provisions of HIPAA.
No comparable provisions.	The above privacy and confidentiality provisions would not preempt more stringent state requirements.
Requires the HHS Secretary, within one year, to issue final regulations to implement the above revisions to the privacy rule, in consultation with the Secretaries of Labor and the Treasury. Provides that the above amendments to the privacy rule will take effect 18 months after enactment.	Requires the HHS Secretary to coordinate implementation of the above privacy and confidentiality provisions with the administration of the HIPAA privacy rule.

Table 1. (Continued).

H.R. 493 (as passed by the House, April 25, 2007)	S. 358 (as reported by the HELP Committee, March 29, 2007)
Interagency Coordination — Section 106 (H.R. 493) Sections 105 and 106 (S. 358)	
Requires the Secretaries of HHS, Labor, and the Treasury, through an interagency memorandum of understanding, to coordinate implementation and enforcement of Title I of this act.	Same provision.
No comparable provisions. [Note: effective date provisions appear in each section of Title I.]	Requires the Secretaries of HHS, Labor, and the Treasury to issue final regulations within one year of enactment. Unless otherwise noted, the amendments made by this Title shall take effect 18 months after enactment.

INDEX

A

B

C

D

E

F

G

L

M

N

O

P

Q

R

S